The Crafter's Recipe Book

The Crafter's Recipe Book

200 new ideas for

decorating objects in

paper, fabric, ceramic, and wood

Jessica Wrobel

MAYWOOD PUBLIC LIBRARY
121 SOUTH 5TH AVE.
MAYWOOD, IL 60153

Q

First published in the United States of America by
Quarry Books, an imprint of
Rockport Publishers, Inc.
33 Commercial Street
Gloucester, Massachusetts 01930-5089
Telephone: (978) 282-9590
Fax: (978) 283-2742

Distributed to the book trade and art trade in the United States by
North Light Books, an imprint of
F & W Publications
1507 Dana Avenue
Cincinnati, Ohio 45207
Telephone: (800) 289-0963

Other Distribution by
Rockport Publishers, Inc.
Gloucester, Massachusetts 01930-5089

ISBN 1-56496-445-0

10 9 8 7 6 5 4 3 2 1

Design: The Design Company

Layout: SYP Design & Production

All photography by Michael Lafferty.

Manufactured in Hong Kong.

Gocco printing recipe included courtesy of Riso-Print Gocco.

The designs shown in the Piercing Metal and Cold Metal Forging recipes are copyrighted images of Millie's Mighty Metal Shop and should be used for educational purposes only.

Publisher's Note

The recipes shown in *The Crafter's Recipe Book* offer many new craft ideas, using a variety of mediums. Always use caution when working with paint, glass, metal, or chemicals. Make sure your work area is well-ventilated and wear protective eye gear, gloves, and a respirator. Follow the manufacturer's safety instructions, and keep chemicals and other toxic substances well out of the reach of children. The author and publisher do not accept any liability for accidents.

Acknowledgments

I would like to thank all the following talented artists and sources who contributed their knowledge, skills, and time to this project:

Kathy Batcheller
Lucinda Cathcart
Charlotte's Web
Ferther and Moore
   Rubber Stamps
Edith Heyck
Bay James

Sam Kimball
Paula Beardell Krieg
Mary McCarthy
Cathy McLaurin
Bridgette Heidi Newfell
Rugg Road Paper
   Company

Jarred Sadowski
Thomas Soderberg
Charlotte Sorsen
Annie A. Spring
Tara Wrobel

Thanks to Martha Wetherill, Shawna Mullen, and Heather Yale at Rockport Publishers for graciously accommodating my crazy schedule while also lending their own talents to the success of the project. Thank you, too, for always including a healthy dose of humor in the proceedings.

Contents

How to Use This Book

Devoted fine crafters are always tucking new ideas, inspirations, and techniques under their belt. Certainly, they never throw anything away. It is for these artists that *The Crafter's Recipe Book* was written. With more than 200 enticing finished pieces, this book illustrates the basic steps needed to transform any project into something completely unexpected.

Divided into three sections, Paper, Fabric, and Other Materials, the book provides a vast resource of new skills to apply to your current medium and the encouragement to branch out into something different. For each technique, there is a list of basic supplies, a photograph of a finished sample and one of the skill in progress, and another finished piece that explores a variation. Step by step directions for techniques that are applicable to multiple mediums are followed by the symbols for Paper, Fabric, and Other Materials (▯ , ▦ , and ▣), and reasonable modification of the procedures may be required. At several points in each chapter there are sections called "Experiments in . . ." that highlight one technique from the previous chapter and explore the design possibilities. Look to these segments for ideas that expand on basic methods.

Before setting to work, it is wise to make sure that you have all the basic tools at hand. Scissors, rulers, pencils, glue, and paintbrushes are all to be expected, but there are some other easy-to-find tools that will make your work progress smoothly. For paper projects, the craft knife and square ruler are invaluable for assuring accurate results. The three essentials in the realm of fabric notions are the fabric marking pen,

rotary cutter, and iron. The pen allows you to easily write, draw, and mark fabric projects and then rinses away when you are through. The rotary cutter looks very much like a pizza cutter and is quick and efficient. The iron is indispensable for keeping the project neat and measurements accurate. In addition, it is always a good idea to keep tweezers and a pair of needle-nosed pliers nearby; they are infinitely useful in grasping small objects, no matter what medium you are working in.

Approach these projects with a few basics rules in mind. Paper and fabric both have a grain line, which is the direction the aligned fibers point. Since these two

materials will fold, crease, and tear more easily with the grain than against it, this characteristic can either help or hinder your progress. Almost all fabrics should be prewashed and dried prior to their use in a project, which removes any sizing and preshrinks the fibers.

The Crafter's Recipe Book takes artists, experienced craftsperson and novice alike, into the amazing world of techniques where layering, manipulating, and decorating transform everyday objects to render them special and unique. Along the way, easy-to-follow instructions serve up new ideas and inspirations that get the creative juices flowing. Take the time to experiment, apply traditional techniques to untraditional mediums and vice versa, and be sure to have fun. ✦

Paper Recipes

Wonderful things happen when you look beyond a coat of paint or a bath of dye to change the appearance of paper. Techniques that manipulate the surface of paper produce intriguing alterations of texture and style and can bring a sculptural aspect to any design.

Although the recipes in this section work equally well for large or small areas, match the characteristics of the material with the look you are seeking. A very supple paper may be well suited for sewing and stitch techniques, while a card-weight paper may respond better to slotting and folding. Be sure to use tools that are appropriate for the size and strength of the paper so you can enhance its beauty without fear of damage. ✦

Layering Paper

Decoupage presents endless possibilities in layered colors, textures, and images, all removed from their expected surroundings and reinstalled in places altogether uncommon.

When relying solely on the unique properties of handmade papers, you can soften the fibers and

layered images form new designs

reconfiguring specialty papers with ease

Decoupage Designs

- Seal each side of the prints with a coat of polyurethane and let dry.
- Carefully cut out the images and arrange them in the desired design.
- Working from the background to the foreground, brush the glue over the back side of each image and press onto the surface. Burnish thoroughly with the brayer. Wipe off any excess glue with a damp sponge. Let the arrangement dry.
- Finish the piece with six to fifteen coats of varnish, depending on its intended frequency of use. Let each coat dry before adding the next, alternating the direction of the strokes for each layer.

Pressing Handmade Papers Together

- Tear or cut one paper into pieces of various shapes and sizes. Soak them in water.
- Select a background paper and soak that in water as well.
- Place a sheet of wool felt on top of a pressing board, and lay the background piece of paper on it. Arrange the colored pieces of paper into the desired pattern on top of the background color.
- Place the other sheet of felt, pressing board, and several weights on the papers and let them sit overnight. Remove the weights, top pressing board, and felt and allow the paper to air-dry.

materials

- brushes
- white craft glue
- small sharp scissors
- craft knife
- color reproductions
- sponge
- brayer
- water-based varnish
- surface or project to decorate
- polyurethane

- pieces of handmade paper
- pressing boards
- sheets of wool felt
- water
- weights

press them back together again in a new design that allows a perfectly flush surface.

A lovely way to layer shapes on top of one another is to capture them between a background and a sheer overlay. This will beautifully mute the intensity of the images.

colorful layers combine elegantly with webbing and gold

Fusible Webbing

- Cut a piece of fusible webbing to the size of the background paper. Place it face down over the paper and iron the webbing into place. Refer to the manufacturer's labeling for more specific directions. Peel away the backing paper of the webbing.
- Arrange the leaves on the background paper and cover with a piece of tulle. Place some wax paper over the tulle to prevent the webbing from sticking to the iron.
- Iron the tulle and leaves into place. Gently peel off the wax paper and trim any overhanging tulle.

- gold gilt leaves
- purple marbled paper
- iron
- fusible webbing
- pink tulle
- wax paper

decoupage

For decoupage art, experiment with mixed subject matter and placement of items. Rearranging elements slightly can drastically affect the overall image of any project, from ornaments to boxes.

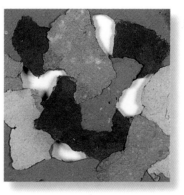

press

Handmade papers were torn apart and then pieced back together in a colorful design. The environmentally friendly appeal of this great recycling technique is a unique finish to any sort of packaging.

fuse

Floating images add an air of whimsy to this design. For a different look, try capturing treasured mementos between two layers.

crafter's tips

- Fusible webbing is available at any fabric store and makes the ease of the work most appealing.
- For a matte finish for the decoupage, build up the first few layers with gloss water-based polyurethane coats and finish with a matte gloss. This will also better protect the project.

These very simple techniques make fine work of everyday items such as tissue paper and confetti. Add even more depth to wrinkling by adding multiple layers of paper or combining different types of paper or found objects together into one piece.

Tissue paper shows up in every gift box and packaged sale, but it is hardly ever given a thought. The inks used to color tissue paper are rarely very well secured to the surface, which makes it easy to manipulate the color variations and how they interact.

layering with wrinkles and folds

designs with a sheer effect

Decorative Tissue Wrinkles

- Brush a generous layer of wallpaper paste onto the turquoise paper.
- Lay the navy tissue paper onto the turquoise paper, allowing it to wrinkle and fold.
- Use your fingers to firmly press all the wrinkles and folds flat. Set this aside overnight to dry thoroughly.
- Brush a coat of acrylic medium over the entire surface of the paper and allow it to dry. This will give the paper sheen and translucency.
- If covering a large area, slightly overlap multiple sheets of tissue paper. Where the sheets meet, fold under and wrinkle the edges so the overall pattern is not disrupted.

Tissue Paper Designs

- Hold the blue tissue paper down and apply it to the white base paper by tearing off small sections with the wet stencil brush. Fill in the background, leaving some areas clear for a secondary color. Set the piece aside for several hours to dry.
- Brush a coat of polyurethane over the blank areas and allow to dry. This will prevent the two ink colors from intermingling too much. Add the second paper in the same manner that the first was added. Let dry.
- Add accents and outline the shapes with the silver pen. Coat the entire surface with polyurethane.

materials

- wallpaper paste
- turquoise paper
- navy tissue paper
- foam brush
- acrylic medium

- white paper
- blue tissue paper
- yellow tissue paper
- stencil brush
- water
- water-based polyurethane
- metallic silver pen

wrinkle

Gold-threaded purple paper, wrinkled over an equally deep purple background, looks like desert drifts of sand when misted with a gold paint.

a delicately layered paper

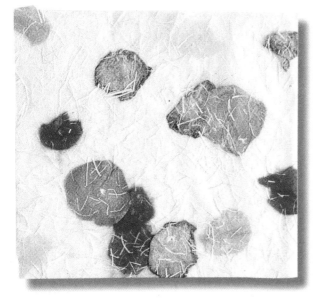

design with tissue

Bright tissue paper tones are muted together, reminiscent of a vivid sunset. The soft gradations of color possible with this technique make it suitable for "painting" and other fine art applications.

Tissue-layered Rose Petals

- Cover the work surface with wax paper and place a sheet of kinwashi paper in front of you. Brush acrylic medium thinly over the paper and scatter a few rose petals and tissue paper pieces across it.
- Brush acrylic medium on a second piece of kinwashi paper and place on top of the first, lining up the edges and capturing the rose petals and tissue paper.
- Cover with wax paper and rub to adhere the layers.
- Carefully remove the wax paper and set layered piece aside to dry.

layer

To mimic ice with tissue layers, substitute maple leaves for rose petals and layer between a sheet of blue tissue paper and a crumpled sheet of frosted vellum.

- 2 sheets kinwashi paper
- wax paper
- acrylic medium
- foam paintbrush
- dried rose petals
- scraps of colored tissue paper cut into petal-size pieces

crafter's tip

▲ Whenever your project incorporates multiple layers of visible materials, be sure to make some samples first to achieve the effect you are looking for.

Besides the obvious appeal of integrating varied elements into a design, weaving paper allows for the muting of a harsh or garish image, presenting it anew in a more refined version. Tearing, however, usually results in a rough and natural look, although many fine papers sport deckled edges.

Salting paper looks beyond the fibers of the earth to create crystalline mounds of texture and depth. Try using salt sculptures to follow the mountains and valleys of a torn piece of paper.

entwine different papers to create something new

add texture with this simple technique

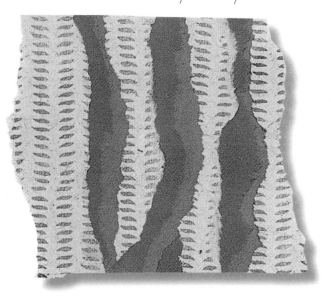

Weaving Paper Images

- Use the ruler and craft knife to cut the image into vertical strips, being sure to leave the top 1/4" (.5 cm) intact.
- Cut the cream paper into strips as well. Make sure they are long enough to travel the width of the image.
- Thread one of the cream strips under the first strip of the image and then over the next. Continue in this manner across the width of the piece.
- Weave the next cream strip into the pattern, this time starting over the first image strip and then under the next. Continue until the image has been completely woven.

Tearing Paper

- Tear the green paper into strips. Repeat with the gold and cream paper. Remember, when tearing along the grain of the paper you will get a straighter, more even line. Going against the grain produces a more varied result.
- Brush a coat of glue over the back side of a green strip and overlap it onto a gold and cream strip. Repeat with the remaining strips of paper in an alternating or random pattern.
- Trim the top and bottom ends with a craft knife and ruler to straighten the edges.

materials

- ruler
- craft knife
- cream paper
- photocopied image

- PVA glue
- green paper
- gold and cream paper
- glue brush
- craft knife
- ruler

weave

A sample exhibits texture achieved by twisting the strips of paper as they were woven together. The beautiful pattern produced would be perfect for a shade or screen.

build layers and dimension in this unusual medium

tear

Tearing paper need not be a straight up-and-down process. This marbled paper was torn into various shapes and then glued back together. The result is the look of marbled stone.

Fixing Salt in Place

○ Color the salts by firmly stirring them with a piece of chalk in a small container. This process will grind the pigment of the chalk into the salt. Repeat for as many colors as you require.

○ Spray a generous coat of adhesive on the paper and pour the salts onto it in the desired pattern. Flip the paper over in one quick motion to dump off any of the salt that did not adhere.

○ Continue adding layers of adhesive and salt until the pattern has been built up to the desired consistency.

salt

Unlike its counterpart in the project, this salt design is cloudy and muted. Salted projects are not great for high-abuse items, but they are the perfect accent for delicate earrings or pendants.

■ table salt

■ colored chalks

■ small containers

■ spray adhesive

■ white paper

crafter's tip

▲ To achieve very straight and true tears, line a ruler up along the tear line before proceeding.

A dense pile of paper carpet is a luxurious addition to any paper craft project, from light-use items like shades and decorative upholstery to books and boxes with a special twist. Shag paper is particularly effective in modern artworks and even in children's storybooks and dollhouses.

Adding a plastic wrap texture to paper creates a glistening, leathery look and is a refined finish for albums, frames, and borders. It is also a perfect way to provide beautiful protection for furniture such as stools and hard-backed chairs.

create a lush pile with paper fibers

A Paper Rug

- Cut your paper into 3/4" (2 cm) strips that are no longer than 5" to 6" (13 cm to 15 cm) long.

- Without creasing it, loosely fold a strip of paper as if you were making a fan. Grasp and twist the bottom of this gathered bundle, forming a paper tuft. Continue this process with each remaining paper strip.

- Thread a generous length of string onto the needle, knotting one end. Pierce through the bottom twist of eight tufts of paper and slide them all the way down to the knot.

- Coil the strung paper around itself so that a dense pile begins to form. On the back side of the piece, make small stitches and tie knots to hold the coils in place. Thread four more tufts of paper onto the string and continue coiling and knotting the threaded paper.

materials

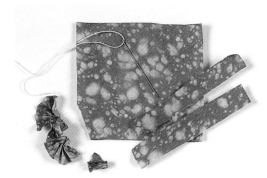

- mustard paper
- lightweight string
- large needle
- craft knife
- ruler
- scissors

pile

Strips of paper with a different color for each side were pleated and stitched onto background paper, creating rows of varying flaps. Try combining different colored papers in one piece for a truly unusual project.

a simple means of adding a leather-like quality

antique

Before applying the acrylic medium to this image, a bit of yellow acrylic paint was mixed in. The effect is an antiqued look that complements an already muted image.

Plastic Wrap Texture

- With the foam brush, apply a very thick coat of acrylic medium to the surface of the image. Point all the brush strokes in the same direction.

- To give the piece a rippled, leather-like texture, lay a sheet of plastic wrap on top of the acrylic medium, and manipulate the surface into a pattern of pleats and folds. Set it aside to dry thoroughly.

- If additional depth is required, repeat the process, adding as many layers of medium as necessary to achieve the desired effect.

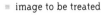

- image to be treated
- acrylic medium
- plastic wrap
- foam brush

crafter's tip

▲ When making paper rugs, it is best to work with a lightweight and pliable paper. This will ensure easy handling and quick results.

Scrape-to-crayon and masking fluid applications add funk or elegance to hand-crafted wrapping papers, cards, and name tags, whether you choose bright colors with a controlled design or muted tones with wild, free-form gestures.

These techniques are exciting ways to approach paper product design. Carving detail into a child's storybook would add visual interest and transform the piece into a treasured heirloom.

Be sure to keep your options open when combining techniques with materials. Surprising results surface when you tackle ordinary design problems with unexpected mediums.

uncovering a hidden design

the liquid "decoder"

Scrape-to-Crayon

- Use the pencil to lightly outline a design on the white paper.
- Color in the design with crayons, making sure the colors are saturated and the surface is completely covered.
- Paint over the entire surface of the decorated paper with a coat of black water-based paint. Allow this to dry for several hours.
- With the knitting needle or another type of stylus, scrape off the black paint in a pattern to reveal the crayon colorings underneath. Be careful not to scrape too hard or you will go through the layer of crayon or the paper itself.

Masking Fluid

- Paint a random design on the white base paper to create the background colors. Allow this to dry.
- Use a paintbrush or calligraphy quill pen to draw a pattern, such as shooting stars, with the masking fluid and let it dry. Immediately wash out the paintbrush as directed on the bottle of masking fluid.
- Brush a coat of black latex paint over the entire surface of the paper and wait for it to dry.
- With your fingers, carefully rub off the masking fluid. You will notice that areas the fluid covered are still the original colors of the painted paper.

materials

- crayons
- white paper
- black acrylic paint
- paintbrush
- knitting needle
- pencil

- masking fluid
- latex paints
- paintbrush
- white paper

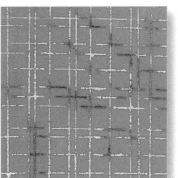

scrape

This scrape-to-crayon design brings to mind the internal workings of a computer with its regular "woven" pattern of lines scraped into a green top coat of paint.

layering and chiseling a design

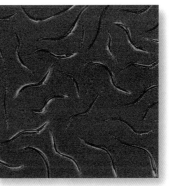

mask

Carefree swirls float over the surface of a shimmering dusty rose and silver paper, creating a charming feeling of whimsy that is wonderful for wrapping paper, diary jackets, and ornaments.

Carving Paper

- Cut sheets of paper to 2" (5 cm) longer than the carving's finished size.

- Brush glue onto the bottom paper and press the next piece on, leaving no air bubbles. Continue gluing papers together until the stack measures at least 1/8" (.25 cm) thick. Dry overnight.

- Clamp the stack of papers down, utilizing the 1" (3 cm) margin on the edges to attach the clamps. Using a sharp, narrow-bladed chisel, carefully hammer out the desired design. Do not apply too much pressure or you will cut through the piece.

- Clean up rough edges with a craft knife, and cut off the margins.

carve

Undefined figures squiggle and squirm across the page in playful unrest. Use paper carvings for box decoration, mirror accents, and story-book characters.

- card-weight paper in a variety of colors
- hammer
- chisel
- C clamps
- PVA glue
- glue brush
- craft knife
- ruler

crafter's tip

▲ When you have finished scraping out crayon designs, brush three coats of water-based polyurethane over the surface, letting each coat dry before adding the next. This will seal the image and protect the design from any future nicks, scrapes, or scratches.

Experiments in Scrape-to-Crayon

 Swirls of three different shades of purple lurk beneath a dusty rose top coat. The resulting rain-like pattern is formed by a series of diagonal dashes. Protect finished pieces with a coat of water-based polyurethane.

 A needle was used to form narrow lines; the broad end of a pair of tweezers carved the wider bands, which display the checkerboard below. Try patterns like this for end papers and dust jackets.

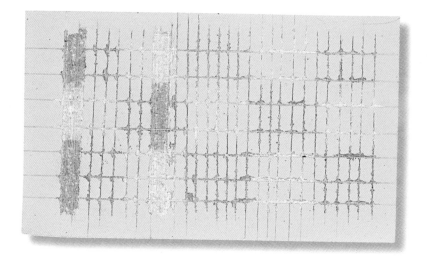

 This scrape-to-crayon design is based on a black background with the color pattern provided by the top coat of paints. The Caribbean colors are accented by the turquoise background paper.

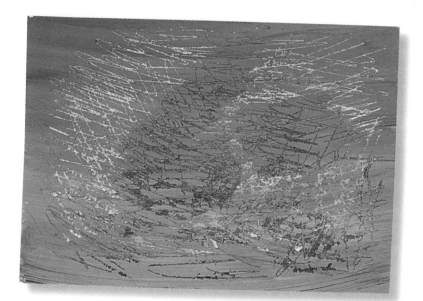

Instead of brushing a flat coat of paint over the black crayon background, this sample features blue and green paint mottled together. Use these papers on frames, trays, and bookmarks.

Wild weather is brought to mind by this freehand design on a murky gray background. Using one of the transfer techniques found on pages 90 to 91, transfer the design to fabrics or other materials.

A traditional black top coat shows off the metallic crayons' irregular plaid pattern below. Experiment with different types of tools as you work with these designs. Needles, knitting needles, and nails all work well.

Manipulating Paper

Folding paper seems too simple to create such varied results. Frequently a three-dimensional project like origami can be adapted into a two-dimensional wonder. Cards, envelopes, and picture frames can all benefit from a simple fold.

Embossing adds dimension and a sculptural quality to paper. Select papers that are supple enough to clearly show the embossed shapes.

fold paper to create fanciful shapes

use a pattern tile to create embossed designs

Folding Paper

○ As you lay out your folding project, remember that it is easier to fold paper parallel to its grain line rather than perpendicular to it. Glue the papers back to back, making sure that the grain of each is pointing in the same direction. Let dry.

○ With a pencil, mark the end points of each fold line on the side of the paper that will be inside the fold.

○ Line up a ruler between the two points and run the dull side of a butter knife along the edge of the ruler and the paper to ensure that the fold line will be clean.

○ Carefully fold the paper along the marked line, creasing it firmly with your thumb. For ready-made folding designs, see the paper folding patterns on page 138.

Star Embossing

○ To make a pattern tile, cut the desired shapes out of chipboard and glue to chipboard backing that is slightly larger than the paper you want to emboss. Let dry.

○ Lay the pattern tile design side up and cover with a sheet of plastic wrap. This will keep the paper you are embossing from sticking to the tile.

○ Lightly brush water on the paper and place on top of the plastic wrap. Cover with a second sheet of plastic wrap, followed by several towels or felts and a pressing board or large book. Stack additional heavy weights on top and leave overnight. Remove paper.

materials

- purple marbled paper
- yellow paper
- ruler
- pencil
- butter knife

- 1/6" chipboard
- PVA glue
- glue brush
- mat knife
- ruler
- towels or felts
- heavy weights or books
- plastic wrap
- paintbrush
- water

Paper fluting, often used on lampshades, can also be displayed on valances. Combine folds and fluting into one piece to bring excitement to a project, and play off the paper's pattern. Work with the fluid curves of the design or stop them in their tracks with a harsh linear fold.

curving paper decoratively

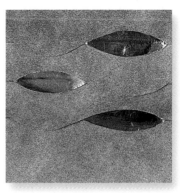

fold

To create new silhouettes, cut paper into shapes around the fold line. Alternating S-curves were cut with a craft knife before creasing the folds, to reveal both sides of the paper when folded.

emboss

A chicken wire pattern was made by embossing and was accentuated by making a rubbing of the wire before pressing.

Fluting

- Determine the placement of each fluted section by lightly marking the end points of the parallel lines across the gold-patterned paper.
- Prebend the fibers between each set of points as described in the Folding Paper recipe. Fold all the marked lines toward the front side of the paper.
- Brush some glue on the back side of the gold paper in the area between the left-hand edge and the first fold line. Press this edge down firmly onto the white paper.
- Continue gluing down every other panel between the fold lines, aligning them on the base paper in such a way that the unglued portion curves into the fluted shape.

flute

Don't be limited by rigid, regular fluting. The gold gilded leaves in this paper give it an earthy feel that is enhanced by the fluting's inconsistent and rumpled appearance. The paper takes on the look of a grove of trees.

- white paper
- gold-patterned paper
- ruler
- pencil
- butter knife
- PVA glue
- glue brush

crafter's tip

▲ The heavier the weight of a paper, the more important it is to mark off and prebend the fibers along a fold line. This will ensure neat, clean, and accurate folds that won't detract from the finished piece.

Quilting with paper is a fabulous way to present a twist when working in traditional or modern applications. The sculptural mounds created by rows of stitching are surprisingly fluid on a somewhat stiff medium.

Indenting, a free-form version of embossing, alters a paper's appearance and texture. Use different tools when designing to achieve various looks, perfect for decorating the covers of albums or desk accessories.

Adding dimension with stitches will challenge your imagination. The lozenge stitch, traditional on fabric, becomes daring when applied to paper.

sewing with paper

decorative imprinting on paper

Quilting Stitches

- Sandwich a layer of quilt batting between a piece of purple paper and a slightly smaller piece of white textured paper.
- With the white paper facing up, slide the stack of papers and batting underneath the foot of the sewing machine. Using a fairly long stitch length, let the texture of the white paper guide you in sewing multiple rows of stitches. Continue until you have filled the paper with the stitched design.
- Clip all the loose threads close to the paper and cut away as much excess batting as possible. Seal the edges of the purple and white papers with glue.

Veining Indentations

- Cut four squares of a soft, thick paper and stack them together. The bottom three layers will create the give required to make visible marks while reinforcing the paper.
- Run the knitting needle along the ruler to form the straight lines of your design. Be sure to press down firmly enough into the paper to leave a strong, heavy line without making tears or punctures.
- Once the design has been indented, cut a piece of maroon paper 1" (3 cm) larger than the white to serve as the base paper and frame. Glue the white paper to the center of the maroon piece.

materials

- purple paper
- thread
- sewing machine
- white textured paper
- quilt batting
- PVA glue
- glue brush

- white flower petal paper
- ruler
- knitting needle
- scissors or craft knife
- gold-threaded maroon paper
- PVA glue
- glue brush

simple smocking creates a raised surface

Smocked and Gathered Paper

- This smocking is formed by sewing together the corner points of 1/2" (1 cm) squares, spaced 1" (3 cm) apart with pencil and ruler on the back of the paper. For a ready-made pattern that you can follow, see the smocking pattern supplied on page 136.
- Crumple paper into a ball and open it up. Repeat until it feels supple.
- Thread a small needle and make a little stitch at the upper left corner of the first square. Make a stitch at the bottom right corner, another at the bottom left corner, and again at the upper right corner to form a stitched *x*.
- Gently pull thread, bringing corners together. Secure with several small stitches. Repeat for remaining squares.

- lightweight fiber paper
- pencil
- ruler
- needle
- thread

quilt

Try using quilted papers on a custom-designed headboard to create a truly unique piece of home decor. Look to the papers themselves or traditional quilting design for ideas and inspiration.

indent

A piece of gold foil paper was indented with a design of tiny waves. The knitting needle used was much smaller than the one in the project and created finer, more detailed lines.

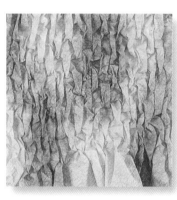

smock

A smocked look is stunning as a finish for presentation folders and paper lanterns or as a border accent for treasured framed items, such as wedding invitations or awards.

crafter's tip

▲ When working with paper, be careful not to make stitches that are too small. The holes left by the sewing needle will serve as perforations, and the paper will tear.

Slotting adds texture to plain papers and can present a curious interruption on printed surfaces. Try layering and folding slotted papers to reveal the paper underneath.

Interest in cutwork is sure to follow slotting. Removing windows in paper adds charm. Use novelty hole-punchers from craft and office supply stores to vary cutwork openings.

Surprising things happen to color intensity when you play with elevation. The checkerboard pattern is regular in color distribution, but with increased height, the colors become more dominant.

simple cuts add texture

intricate designs are formed quickly

Slotting Patterns

- Select a sturdy paper to ensure that the intended pattern will be visible in the finished piece.
- With the ruler and pencil, carefully measure out and mark the pattern of slot marks on the back side of the paper.
- Use the ruler as a guide to cut along the pencil markings with the craft knife. For this particular pattern of peaks, it is easiest to make all the cut marks in one direction before making the others.
- Adjust the slots and tabs as needed. These peaks were folded slightly forward.

Cutwork with Freezer Paper

- On the dull side of the freezer paper, draw out the pattern to be cut into the burgundy paper. For an easy alternative to drawing the design, copy, cut out, and trace the cutwork pattern supplied on page 137. Remember, the end result of the cutwork design will be the mirror image of the drawing.
- Set the iron to a low temperature and iron the freezer paper, shiny side down, to the back side of the burgundy paper.
- Carefully cut out the design with the craft knife as marked on the freezer paper.
- When the design is completely cut out, gently peel the freezer paper off the back of the burgundy paper and discard.

materials

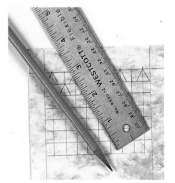

- rose marble paper
- ruler
- craft knife
- pencil

- pencil
- freezer paper
- craft knife
- burgundy paper
- iron

slot

A slotted piece layers two different marbled papers. The top piece is slotted and folded back on itself to reveal the back side of the paper.

bring paper to new heights with this technique

cutwork

Layers of cutwork designs create the feel of snow falling behind a stained glass window. Both this technique and slotting are great for shades and place mats.

Paper Elevations

- On the foam core, use the pencil and ruler to mark the base pattern of your design. A grid was formed for this checkerboard pattern.
- Cut the mottled papers into shape with the craft knife. Cut the chipboard into numerous pieces slightly smaller than the paper pieces. These will be used to stack beneath the papers to achieve varying elevations.
- Glue the chipboard stacks of differing heights to the foam core base as dictated by your design.
- Glue the paper pieces to the top of each stack.

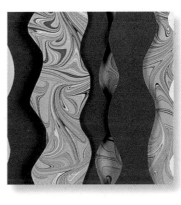

elevate

Graceful waves seem to be even more in motion when layered over one another. Try this technique in dioramas, cards, and even architectural finishes for a playroom.

- mottled silver paper
- mottled rose paper
- PVA glue
- glue brush
- foam core
- chipboard
- ruler
- pencil
- craft knife

crafter's tip

▲ Use wire instead of chipboard to create paper elevations. Not only can you affect the height of a paper, you can bend it askew for an added twist.

These simple, beautiful techniques give paper texture and dimension, and different looks can be achieved with regular or random designs. Tight curls and small beads tame the overall feel of a piece, while large, loose swirls create a more casual appearance.

A piece of paper can be defined by crumpling specific sections. Once you have crumpled a portion of the paper, it will be slightly smaller than when you started. Adding folds and/or flutings to the uncrumpled section will compensate for the area loss.

rolling paper into beads

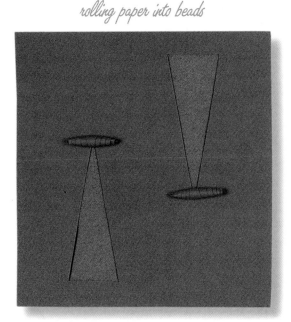

making paper spirals

Self-beading Paper

- On the back side of the violet paper, mark three points to make a triangular strip that will form the bead.

- Leaving enough of the tip intact so the triangle cannot be removed, use a craft knife to cut along the lines of the marked points.

- From the front of the paper, slip the wide end of one triangle between the legs of the cotter pin, and tightly roll the paper toward its narrow point. Secure the new bead with glue. Repeat.

- Brush some glue over the back side of the beaded paper and press it onto the green paper, making sure there are no air bubbles.

Curling

- On the back side of the blue paper, draw the outlines of the shapes to be cut out.

- Use the craft knife to cut along the drawn lines. Leave one side of the shape uncut and attached to the paper.

- Apply some glue to the surrounding areas of the blue paper's back side. Press this down onto the yellow marbled paper. Do not allow the cutouts to become glued to the paper.

- Roll the cut strips of paper around the pencil tightly. Remove the pencil and tug gently on the end of the paper to telescope its curves out into a spiral.

materials

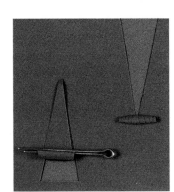

- ruler
- pencil
- craft knife
- cotter pin
- PVA glue
- glue brush
- green paper
- violet paper

- pencil
- craft knife
- glue brush
- PVA glue
- blue paper
- yellow marbled paper

bead

Not only do these beads embellish the paper, but the pattern in which they were cut lends itself beautifully to this star-burst design.

curl

This normally subdued paper embedded with flower petals takes on a whole new attitude with large, easygoing swirls. Arranged in alternating directions, these curls add texture and dimension.

crumple

Crumpling adds shadow and intrigue to the simplest of papers. This golden yellow sample incorporates folds, slots, and crumples.

create decorative paper pictures with wrinkles

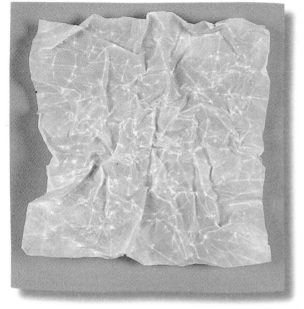

Crumpled Vellum

○ Select a light- to medium-weight vellum to work with. Papers that are very thick tend to tear and puncture as they are crumpled.

○ Wad the paper as you would if you were throwing it away. Open it up and repeat until you have the desired texture. The more you wad the piece, the softer and more supple it will become.

○ On the back side of the crumpled vellum, spray a coat of adhesive. Center the vellum over the green paper and press down gently to adhere the two together. Be careful not to smooth out any of the crumplings.

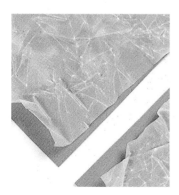

■ vellum

■ green paper

■ spray adhesive

crafter's tip

▲ Try laminating a third paper to the back side of beaded or curled paper to introduce a new design option. Be careful not to add to the thickness too much, or the project will become difficult to handle.

aces needn't be confined to your shoes. Fun finishes like these are great for closures on gift cards, binders, and books. Try a more refined look by combining beautiful specialty papers with fine ribbon lacings.

Jump rings make dashing attachments to fine paper projects, but other options are endless. Experiment with string, buttons, or safety pins to make runners, shades, or curtains.

Paper string is easy to make, and it will expand your expectations of paper. Try combining different colored papers for a variegated effect.

fashion finishing for paper

jump rings connect colorful swatches of paper

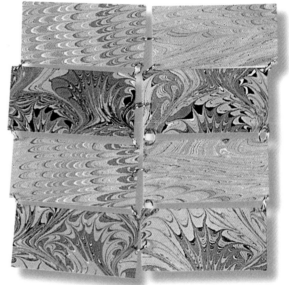

Grommeting and Lacing

- Measure and mark off the points where the grommets are to be applied along one side of two pieces of paper. Cut a small "x" over each point with the knife.
- From the front side of the paper, insert the shank of the grommet through the "x" cut of one point.
- On the back side, center the grommet tool over the grommet and smack it with the hammer to flatten the grommet. This will secure it to the paper. Repeat with each of the remaining points.
- Lace the two pieces of paper together by threading the shoelace through the grommets.

Joining Paper with Jump Rings

- Cut the paper into rectangles. For this project, there are four of each color measuring 1" (3 cm) by 2" (5 cm).
- Lay out the paper in the desired pattern, and punch a hole with the needle in each jump ring location. Do not place the hole too close to the edge or the paper may tear.
- Link the papers together with the jump rings. Using the needle-nosed pliers will make handling the small pieces more comfortable.
- Assemble the pattern by working one row at a time, and then go back to join each row to the others.

materials

- grommets
- grommeting tool
- hammer
- paper
- pencil
- ruler
- craft knife
- shoelace

- green marbled paper
- purple marbled paper
- 7 mm gold jump rings
- needle
- needle-nosed pliers
- ruler
- pencil
- craft knife

grommet

Alternate the placement of the front of the grommet on both sides of the paper. This will allow you to fold back the paper to create a more tailored look.

reconfigure the format of paper by twisting

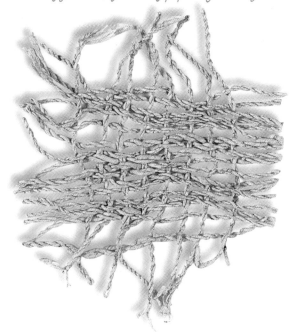

join with wire

This sample uses wire instead of jump rings to link tiny squares of paper together. The result is a very sculptural effect that looks slightly windblown.

Paper String Designs

○ Along its longest side, cut the tissue paper into strips that are 1" (3 cm) wide.

○ While holding one end of a strip down firmly, twist the other end until the entire piece has been twisted tightly enough to curl back on itself.

○ Bring the two ends together while keeping a firm grasp on the middle of the strip. Allow the strip to twist around itself into a two-ply string.

○ Weave the strings together in the classic under/over basket weave pattern.

○ Apply a dot of glue with the needle at the string intersections to secure the pieces in place.

twist

Frog closures made from paper string are another option for paper fasteners. These were made exactly the same way as their fabric counterparts.

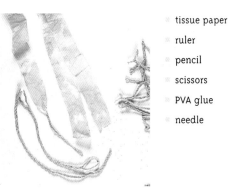

▨ tissue paper

▨ ruler

▨ pencil

▨ scissors

▨ PVA glue

▨ needle

crafter's tip

▲ When making paper string, be sure to use a lightweight paper that can be manipulated easily.

Any humid, summer day will cause graceful waves in your books and magazines, but who would have thought that a summer nuisance could produce such splendid results? Different types of paper absorb water in distinct ways, and experimenting with combinations can create many varied results.

The ghost-like images and translucent ambience of acrylic transfers give a unique character to projects. Try layering the images over reflective surfaces such as mylar or metallic origami papers. An application with a light source behind it is particularly beautiful.

Corrugating paper is a simple way to add structure and uniformity to a paper, especially a patterned piece such as the layered kinwashi paper used here. Customize the size of the ridges of corrugation by adhering larger diameter dowels to a cardboard backing to use as the press. Create multi-sized corrugated ridges by forming the pattern with several sizes of dowels, making sure that each side of the press mirrors the other.

soak paper strips in water to produce graceful waves

make translucent transfers of paper treasures

Soaking and Warping Paper Strips

- Cut the white paper into 3/4" (2 cm) strips. Stack the strips in a pile, and lay the stack on its side.
- Use the needle and string to sew the stack of paper strips together. For this sample, the strips were sewn together at both ends and the middle.
- Prepare a bowl of purple dye as directed on its package, and soak the sewn papers overnight.
- Remove the paper from the dye bath, and let it air-dry until it is no longer dripping. To create the soft, weathered edges, run the paper through a clothes dryer to finish the drying process. Finally, chenille yarn is banded around the ends for added color.

Image Transfers Using Acrylic Medium

- Select an image you created or collected. It must be on paper, and it will eventually be destroyed. Photocopied photographs will also work.
- Brush acrylic over the image, keeping the strokes in one direction. Let dry.
- Continue until there are at least five coats. Alternate the direction of the strokes for each layer. The more layers there are, the stronger the transfer will be.
- Once dry, place the piece face down in a pan of water. Soak for several minutes.
- Gently remove the paper from the back side of the acrylic.
- Remove the film from the water and let dry.

materials

- white paper
- purple dye
- large sewing needle
- white string
- chenille yarn
- bowl
- craft knife
- ruler
- clothes dryer

- acrylic medium
- foam brush
- image
- shallow pan
- water

warp

Discarded books take on new life when slashed into sections of varying heights and soaked in water. The thick, warped panels make wonderful bottom linings for boxes or, on a larger scale, great wall panels.

a corrugated cardboard press gives smooth papers texture

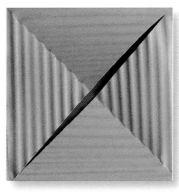

transfer

Romantic couples are fun and dreamy backed with a lovely red tone. The clarity of these transfers allows for layering of multiple images.

Pressure Corrugation

○ Make a corrugation press by threading wooden dowels into corrugated cardboard. Cut the dowels to equal the width of the cardboard. Insert a dowel into each hollow ridge of the corrugated cardboard.

○ Center a sheet of paper on top of the corrugated side of the press.

○ Place the other piece of the press, corrugation side down, on top of the paper so that the ridges of one piece fit into the grooves of the other.

○ Starting at the bottom, roll with a rolling pin, pressing down firmly. Remove the paper from the corrugation press. For thicker papers, dampen with a little water first.

press

Ornate and geometric, the paper shown was folded before being run through the corrugation press. It was then cut in half and layered over a background color.

- 2 sheets corrugated cardboard
- 1/8" (.25 cm) wooden dowels
- rolling pin
- sturdy scissors
- paper

crafter's tip

▲ Image transfers work best from color photocopies, so be sure to transfer photographs or magazine images to this medium before proceeding with the technique.

Experiments in Stitching Paper

Paper takes on the look of lace when cut work is combined with a stitched edging.

A herring-bone stitch encases and enhances the impact of gold ribbons. This design is particularly effective as edging on the covers of wedding or anniversary albums.

Use all-over stitching to create a repetitive texture that dramatically changes the look and feel of the paper.

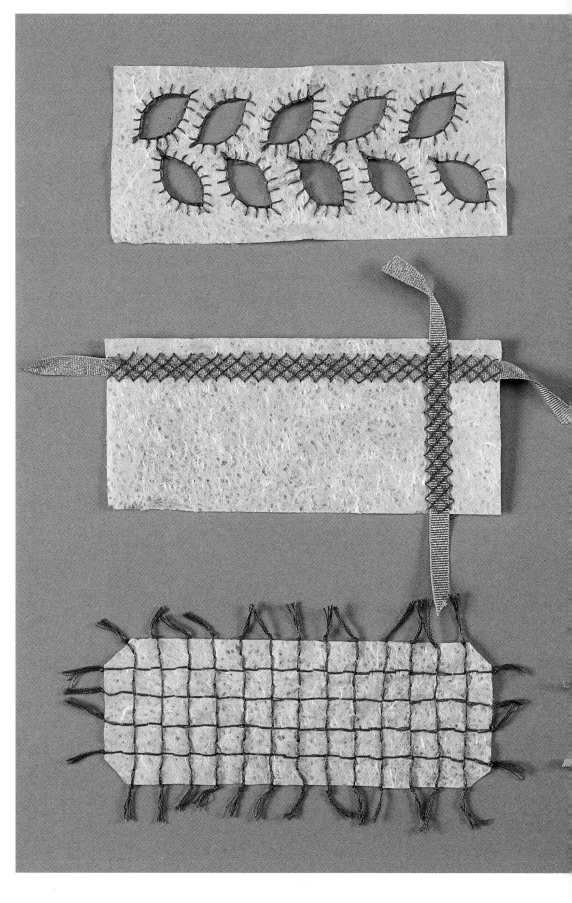

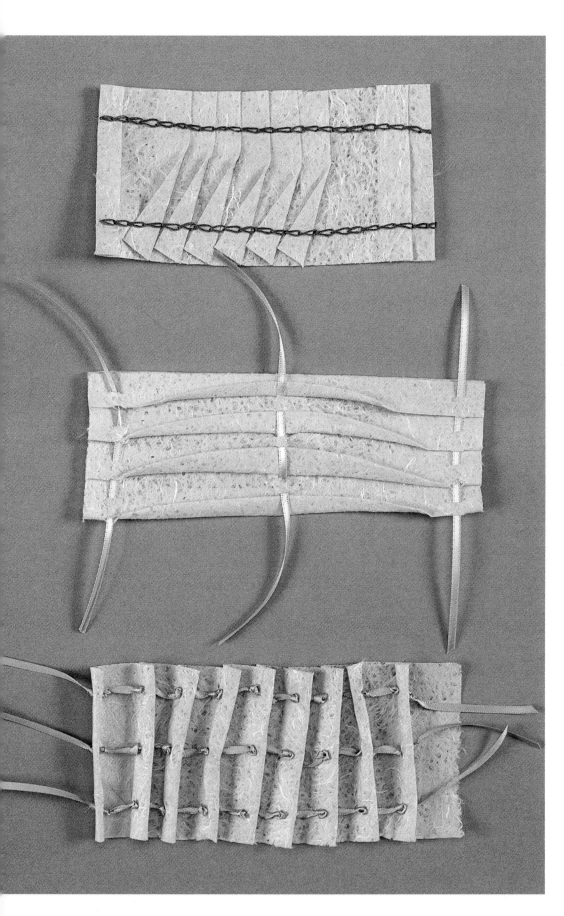

A series of tucks, pleats, and folds are held in place with a chain stitch.

This sample plays with the same principal as above, but relies on ribbon stitching to hold horizontal folds in place.

A series of knots on several lengths of ribbon hold paper in a fluted pattern that is well suited for decorating lampshades and lanterns.

Paper Surface Finishes

Crayon batik transforms the results of a childhood medium into a sophisticated fine art, rich in depth and color. Experiment with different papers to find the ones best suited for this technique.

There are unlimited ways to change paper's appearance. A traditional technique like marbling

crackled crayon designs

Crayon Batik

- Draw a picture or pattern on the paper in crayon. Color in the entire surface of the paper very densely so none of the paper shows through.
- To crack the surface, wad the paper into a tight ball, then unfurl it. Brush a thinned coat of paint over the entire surface. Do not let paint dry.
- Lay the piece on top of the wax paper, and sponge the paint off the crayon.
- Place the design face down on a sheet of scrap paper. Stack another piece of scrap paper on top of that. Press with a warm iron, but do not use a sliding motion.

a frozen twist on a traditional technique

Ice Marbling

- Make up the marbling bath as described on the packet of methyl cellulose. Pour the mixture into a shallow container and place it in your freezer.
- Mix the alum as directed and sponge it over the paper. Let dry.
- Once the bath is frozen, remove it from the freezer and allow it to defrost until it is slushy.
- Apply the inks to the surface of the bath with squirt bottles. Configure the desired ink patterns with a stylus.
- Lay your paper face down onto the surface of the bath, then remove it and rinse. Hang to dry.

materials

- crayons
- paper
- iron
- acrylic paint
- water
- paintbrush
- sponge
- wax paper
- scrap paper

- freezer
- methyl cellulose
- water
- ammonia
- shallow tray
- sponge
- alum
- paper
- marbling acrylics
- stylus
- squirt bottles

becomes new when the bath is frozen; this causes sharp edges to form instead of the usual ethereal swirls.

The x-ray-like quality of bubble marbling is fascinating and unexpected. Light imprints are perfect additions to books, cards, and building blocks.

soap suds imprint delicate images

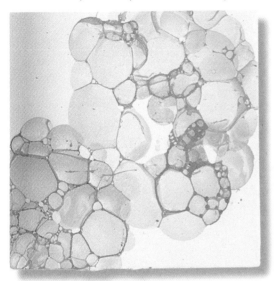

Bubble Marbling

◦ Mix a solution of liquid dishwashing detergent and water in roughly a four-to-one ratio. The consistency should be that of light cream.

◦ Thoroughly stir one color into the solution to reach the desired intensity. In separate bowls, create additional colors the same way.

◦ With a straw, blow bubbles into the first color. Working one small area at a time, quickly lay the paper face down onto the bubbles and remove it. Let it sit for a moment so any bubbles remaining on the surface of the paper pop, and the paper has a chance to dry. Continue adding more colors in the same manner.

■ liquid dishwashing detergent

■ shallow bowls

■ straws

■ intense colors such as marbling inks or tempera

■ paper

■ water

batik

Instead of the abstract design of the project piece, this sample presents a clearly defined image. Papers like this are a gorgeous addition to books, binders, and signs.

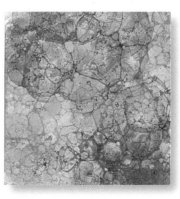

marble

This paper was rocked back and forth as it was laid into its bath. This created light lines, as if the paper were under rippling water.

bubble

Multiple layers of color were applied to this bubble marbling piece to create a dense pattern. Try combining this technique with traditional marbling methods.

crafter's tip

▲ Leftover bubble marbling mixtures can be kept in airtight containers for one to two years.

aste papers are "blank slates," perfect for tackling your own design schemes. The translucent, malleable, and colorful nature of the paste allows for wild interpretations or sophisticated constructions.

The unique impressions left by the plastic wrap's crystalline patterns will add a jeweled or wintery flair to any project. With practice you will be able to exert more control over the fold of the plastic, ensuring a truly unusual design.

Spray paints, easily obtained at hardware, craft, and art supply stores, are an easy and inexpensive way to experiment with paper. They are available in a wide variety of colors, including many different types of metallic finishes.

colored flour paste is the basis for free-form designs

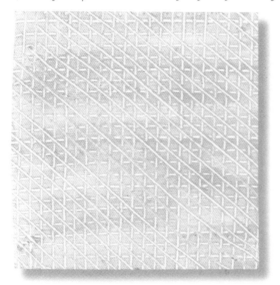

plastic wrap makes crystalline formations

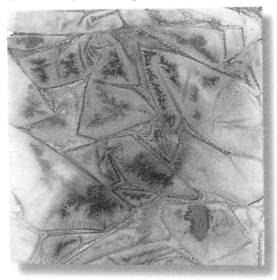

Colored Paste Papers

- Add 2 tablespoons of flour to 2 cups of cold water. Let sit until there are no lumps.
- Stirring constantly, bring the flour mixture to a boil over medium heat. Remove from the burner, and allow it to thicken to a paste as it cools. The mixture should be at room temperature before continuing.
- Mix in an acrylic paint until the desired color is achieved. Brush the paste generously onto the surface of the paper.
- While the paste is wet, drag the styling comb through to create a pattern. Set aside until dry. The color of the acrylic paint, when dry, will lighten a bit.

Crystal Paper Effects

- Brush water over the entire surface of the paper. Carefully add strokes of the paints, allowing them to spread out on the water base.
- Cut a piece of plastic wrap larger than the size of the paper. Lay it down on top of the piece, allowing it to wrinkle and fold. This will capture pockets of ink that will produce the crystal-like images.
- Set the wrapped piece aside for a couple of days to dry thoroughly before carefully removing the plastic wrap.
- Allow any residual dampness on the paper to dry before using the paper.

 materials

- flour
- water
- pot
- stove
- spoon
- white paper
- green acrylic paint
- styling comb
- foam brush

- white paper
- watercolors or acrylic paints
- plastic wrap
- water
- paintbrush

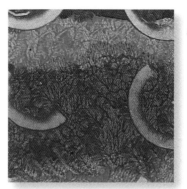

paste

This variation combines two colors of paste applied to the paper by stippling. A larger piece would show a regular pattern of Cs streaming across the page.

create soft color transitions

crystal

Warmer tones were cooled down by the addition of ground silver pigments sprinkled over the wet paints before the plastic wrap was applied. Try using other additives at that stage to vary the results even more.

Gradating with Spray Paint

○ Tape the paper to the cardboard so you have something to hold onto while applying the paint to the paper. This will also help keep your hands clean.

○ Hold the board with the paper vertically. With one color of paint, spray straight down from the top of the board. Allow this to dry before continuing.

○ Rotate the board 180 degrees and spray the other color of paint straight down towards the first color. This will create a paper with strong colors at each end and a blending of the two in the middle. Allow the second color to dry.

spray paint

Textured paper was crumpled into a ball and then pulled apart before applying the two colors of paint. Wrinkles and folds accept the paint differently and cause valleys of varying colors.

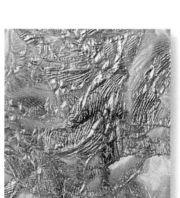

▪ yellow spray paint

▪ silver spray paint

▪ paper

▪ cardboard

▪ tape

crafter's tip

▲ Store unused paste paint in the refrigerator to extend its life. Paste that is left at room temperature will mold quickly.

Piercing beautifully adds texture to paper. Combine different sizes of needle holes to form patterns. Piercing from both sides of the paper will also produce interesting texture variations.

Piercing will inspire you to sew on paper; sculpting with stitches is a wonderful design challenge. For stitching ideas, turn to Experiments in Stitching Paper.

Studs and stones add further texture and dimension to paper. Use them to decorate fancy albums or book covers, although they work equally well on headboards, valances, and frames.

bring texture and light to the surface of paper

metallic thread adds sparkle

Pierce-pattern Paper

∘ Brush an even coat of glue over the back of a sheet of 1/4" (.5 cm) graph paper and attach to the underside of the paper you want to pierce. The graph paper will serve as a guide for even piercing placement.

∘ With a pencil, mark a checkerboard pattern on the graph paper. Each square of the checkerboard should measure 1" x 1" (3 cm x 3 cm).

∘ Pierce through the graph side of the paper, using a large needle to punch the outline of each checkerboard.

∘ Fill in the alternate squares of the pattern with evenly spaced rows of piercings.

Silver-stitch Paper

∘ This card, trimmed with a traditional feather-stitch pattern (see Recipe Resources for more instruction on sewing stitches), uses silver embroidery floss on a mottled rose and silver card-stock paper.

∘ Before you begin, sew a few stitches on a scrap of the paper to make sure it is strong enough to withstand stitching. If the paper tears, try again with a smaller needle.

∘ On the back of the paper, outline the pattern with either small needle punches or pencil marks.

∘ Start the stitching from the back side of the paper so the knots securing the threads will not be visible on the front of the piece.

materials

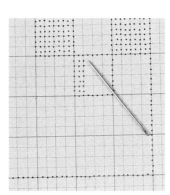

- large needle
- PVA glue
- 1/4" (.5 cm) graph paper
- glue brush
- turquoise paper
- pencil
- ruler

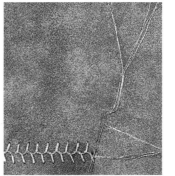

- mottled rose and silver paper
- silver embroidery floss
- sewing needle
- scissors

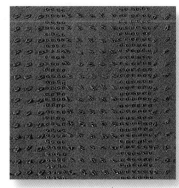

pierce

Openings made with a large upholstery needle were paired alongside a striped pattern of holes created by a bookbinder's needle.

silver costume jewels add sparkle to paper

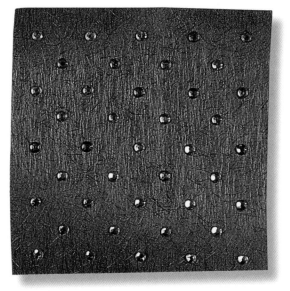

stitch

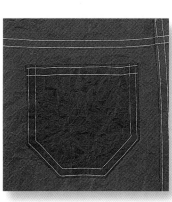

The design of this paper denim pocket is playfully stitched with the traditional gold thread detailing of a favorite pair of blue jeans.

Rhinestone Studding

- Use the ruler and pencil to mark off each point on the paper where a stud will be adhered. In this sample, the points were marked with a dot of white paint for easy visibility.

- On the back side of a rhinestone, place a small drop of glue with the needle. Press it down firmly onto one of the marked points. Be careful not to use too much glue, or it will seep out from behind the stud as it is pressed to the paper.

- Apply a rhinestone to each point in the same manner and set the piece aside to dry.

stud

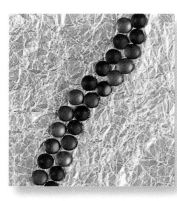

A crumpled gold paper swatch is whimsically bejeweled with variously colored studs. Arranged in a swirling, free-form design, this piece announces a casual royalty.

- rhinestones
- PVA glue
- needle
- maroon paper
- ruler
- pencil

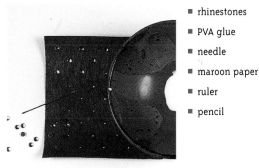

crafter's tip

Many types of studs, snaps, and other embellishments can be clamped directly onto the paper. These pieces usually have a front and a back piece that line up on either side of the paper, so that when one piece is pushed through the paper, prongs from one will latch into the other. These studs or snaps are especially suited for heavier papers that resist tearing.

Not surprisingly, vegetable dyes produce a wide range of earthy tones. The organic colors are perfect accents to recycled products like packaging and stationery.

Curly noodles have a recognizable squiggle shape that transforms a quiet paper into one with sizzle. Macaroni art is not something you need to grow out of.

Sometimes flecking water over solid-color paper brings out unexpected color underneath, such as the muted blue purple in the variation. Even in the world of paper, beauty is not only skin-deep.

a garden palette

painting with pasta

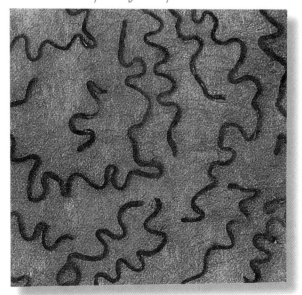

Dyeing with Vegetables

- Shred the beet with the grater.
- Place half of the grated beet into the cheesecloth and squeeze the juice into a small container. Tie up the cheesecloth sack and put it into the juice container. Add water to cover the sack.
- Put the rest of the shredded beet into a cooking pot and cover with water. Bring to a boil and simmer for several minutes without letting all the water cook off. Remove the pot from heat and let cool.
- Apply the dyes to your paper with a paintbrush. Note the raw juice's vivid purple-red versus the cooked liquid's ruddy yellow-brown.

Noodle Masks

- Place the noodles in a bowl of hot water and let soak until they are pliable. Drain the water and set the noodles aside until they feel sticky.
- Arrange the noodles in a random pattern, pressing them down firmly so they have full contact with the paper.
- From directly above the paper, spray a coat of paint. As soon as it is dry, take the noodles off. If you leave the noodles until they are completely dried out, they will tear the paper as they are removed.
- Gently rub the paper with your fingertips to dislodge any remaining traces of the noodles.

materials

- one beet
- cooking pot
- stove
- vegetable grater
- cheesecloth
- string
- water
- paintbrush
- small containers
- paper

- Curly noodles
- hot water
- bowl
- maroon paper
- gold spray paint

flecks on tissue paper for a decorative effect

Water Staining

○ Select a paper with a color that runs when it is wet; tissue paper is excellent in this respect. If your project requires a heavier paper, but you want the look of tissue, glue it to a card-stock piece to stabilize it.

○ Dip the stippling brush in a glass of water and run your finger over the bristles to fleck tiny droplets of water onto the tissue paper. Where the droplets hit the paper, the ink will be "pushed" away, forming circles of bleached paper.

○ Continue splashing water over the tissue paper until an overall design has been formed. Allow this to dry before using.

- brown tissue paper
- stippling brush
- glass of water

dye

The flesh of an onion will cook down to a pale yellow color, while the skin of the onion produces a burnt-orange dye. They are paired with glittery gold accents.

noodles

The confetti appearance of this noodle mask was produced by applying the noodles to a multi-colored base paper and then spraying on coats of several different colors. More noodles were added between each coat of paint.

stain

Stargazing is easy for this silver moon; the white and blue specks were brought out by water applied with a squirt bottle. The moon was blocked out with a cardboard template so the water would not reach that area.

crafter's tips

▲ Experiment with different types of mordants when working with vegetable dyes. The resulting color produced with the use of each one will vary slightly.

▲ Different parts of a vegetable can result in very diverse hues. For example, the leaves of a beet will create a green dye.

Candied paper is a great accent for party place cards and cake boards. Add some candied flowers or foliage to a piece for a festive look.

Nothing may be more common than the office photocopier, and if you are willing to experiment, wonderful things will happen. Remember that many machines will allow you to enlarge or reduce the image as well.

These faux stained glass pieces make exciting window hangings or ornaments. Display them in a situation where they have a light source behind them.

sugared accents create paper confections

put office tools to work in the art studio

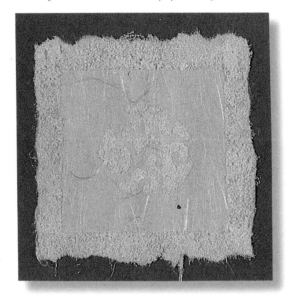

Candied Paper

- Tear the edges of the green paper to give it a deckled edge.
- For the center design, draw your pattern on the card stock and cut it out. Remember that the internal cut areas will be sugared.
- Lay the stencil on top of the green paper and lightly brush egg white over the exposed area. Remove the template and sprinkle sugar over the egg white. Shake off any excess that does not adhere. Repeat for any other sugared areas.
- Glue the candied green paper to the center of a slightly larger piece of plum paper.

Fabric Photocopying

- Select an assortment of objects that will work well together as a collage. This can include two- and three-dimensional items such as papers, fabrics, jewelry, and watches. Rearrange them until you achieve a configuration that is visually pleasing.
- Carefully sketch out the arrangement so that it may be quickly reproduced when you get to a photocopier.
- Make the photocopy as usual, but take time to play with the intensity of the inks in the reproduction. This sample makes use of a color copier, but a black and white copier may be utilized as well.

materials

- card-weight paper for stencil
- green paper
- plum paper
- egg white
- paintbrush
- pencil
- craft knife
- PVA glue
- sugar

- photocopier
- fabric and paper remnants
- scissors
- paper
- pencil

candied

A candied paper design takes its cue from the pattern of the paper. Certain areas of the marbling were brushed with egg white to accept the sugar.

use acrylic transfers to fashion stained glass images

photocopy

To create this sample, various images were copied onto clear acetate so they could be layered on top of one another before finally being printed onto an antique vellum.

stained glass

Copper wire forms the finishing touches on this piece of faux stained glass. The image was already so appropriate for the desired decorative glass effect that it was left to stand on its own.

Faux Stained Glass

- Make acrylic transfers of the images as described on page 36. Be sure to apply a rather thick coat of the acrylic medium.
- Cut the images into shape as the design requires. Lay them out in a pattern in front of you; it may be helpful to sketch out the pattern to use as a guide. Make sure that the edges of the pieces are touching one another.
- Use the foil tape to join the pieces, being sure to burnish the surface thoroughly with your fingers.
- Form a border of tape around the edges of the piece.

- images
- acrylic medium
- foam brush
- water
- shallow pan
- metal foil tape
- scissors
- paper
- pencil

crafter's tip

- To prevent scratching the glass of a photocopier with hard items in your design, arrange the pieces face down in the plastic portion of a box picture frame. Use towels or foam to hold everything in place.

The brayer technique is a masterful yet easy way to quickly cover large areas with color. The project's muted and cloudy effects suggest ethereal matters, while the grid of the variation creates a semblance of order.

Gravestone rubbings from childhood never looked this good. Patience and a steady hand can turn a grade school technique into a sophisticated art form.

Any piece is easily transformed using the crackle texture method. Producing a country or old money appearance, the results of this application are bound to be treasured.

rolling magical designs onto paper

create fun textures within a surface

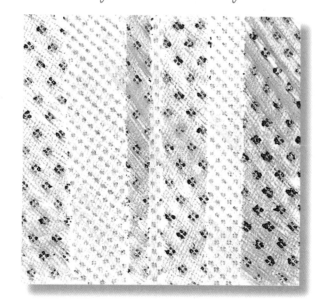

Coloring with the Brayer

○ Roll the brayer over the surface of the ink pad, generously coating it with color.

○ Gently roll the brayer onto the paper, making sure to move the tool in multiple directions. The harder you press, the more distinct the line left by the edge of the roller will be.

○ To remove excess ink on the brayer, roll it over the scrap paper repeatedly. Be sure to do this each time you change ink colors.

○ Continue adding colors in this manner. In this swatch, green ink was applied first and then various shades of blue were added in layers.

Rubbed Stripes of Color

○ Carefully select textured patterns to create the rubbed design. Keep in mind the proportions of the finished piece. Here, various sides of a vegetable grater are used to achieve several different textures.

○ With the tape, mask off sections of paper to isolate areas of crayon markings. Align the paper over the grater. Firmly color over the paper, allowing the crayon to jump over or sink into the markings of the pattern.

○ For this sample, stripes of paper were alternately masked off and rubbed with different colors on different sides of the grater.

materials

■ brayer
■ ink pads
■ white paper
■ scrap paper

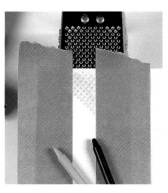

■ white paper
■ crayons
■ textured patterns (a vegetable grater)
■ painter's tape

brayer

Before the brayer was inked up, removable tape was applied to the brayer to mask out an uneven diamond pattern. The tape was then removed before rolling the brayer across the paper. For additional layers, reapply the tape and re-ink the brayer.

presenting an aged elegance

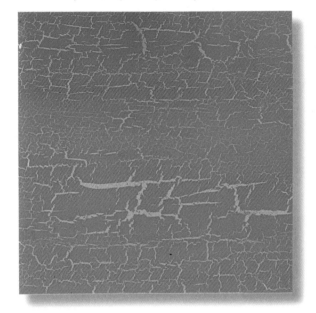

rubbing

Time ignores convention in these pencil rubbings that travel in an unordered fashion. Try doing rubbings with colored soap to make your own presoaped towelettes.

Crackle Texture

- Brush a coat of paint over the surface of the paper. This is the color that will show through the crackled top coat. Set aside to dry overnight.
- Apply the crackle medium to the paper in the same manner. Make sure that the medium is thoroughly dry before continuing.
- With quick strokes, brush the top layer of paint over the crackle medium, being careful not to go over the same area twice. As the paint dries, the cracks will appear.

crackles

Unlike the country look of the project, this sample seems much more regal. There are two layers of crackled paint over the gold base coat.

- white paper
- purple and blue acrylic paints
- paintbrush
- crackle medium

crafter's tips

- Try applying stickers to the brayer before inking it up to achieve a variety of fun shapes and patterns.
- When using the crackle texture technique, the thicker the final coat of paint, the bigger and wider the cracks will be.

Experiments in Paste Paper

 Blue and purple tones are combined to form a crystalline surface, formed by ragging with a plastic grocery bag. The more paint mixed into the paste, the heavier the resulting images will seem.

 A fantasy marble paste paper was finished with several coats of glossy water-based polyurethane. Try malachite or wood patterns to decorate hanging wall panels or "tiled" coffee tables.

 Paste paints are very similar in nature to decorative painting glazes and can be used to create similar effects, such as this green marble.

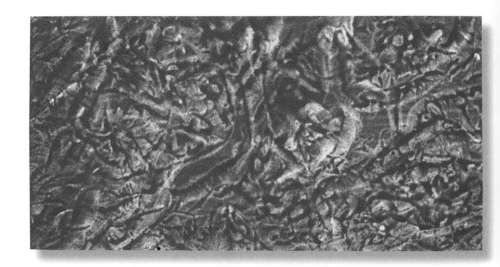

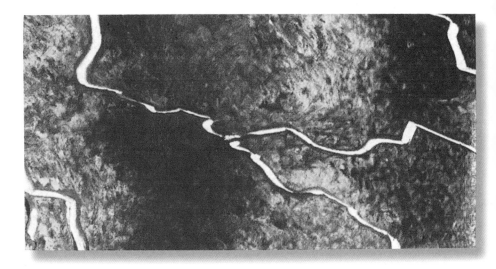

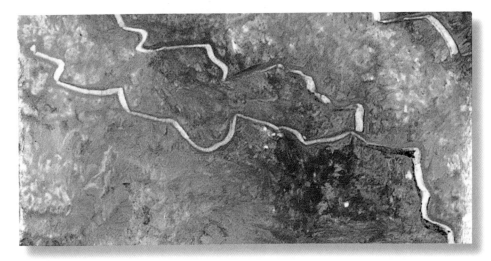

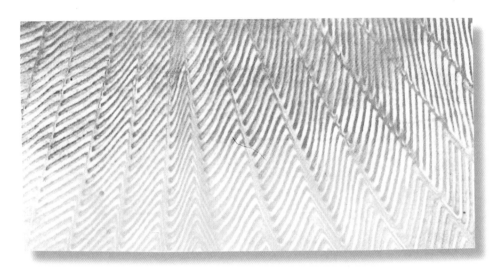

Two colors of paste paint that are mottled together form rays that suggest summer sunsets. The design was made with a jerking motion of an adhesive spreader.

An alternating line pattern was made with the tip of a chopstick. Paste papers are perfect for book covers, boxes, and portfolios.

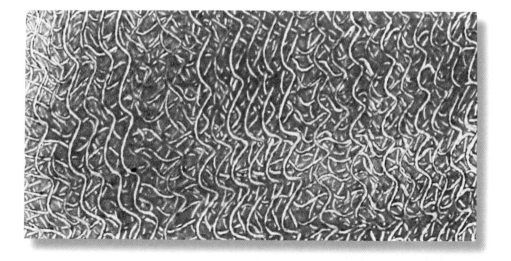

Random squiggles with a hair styling comb create a high-energy design. The flour paste provides the translucency, suspending the paints and allowing the pattern to be scraped down to the clean paper surface.

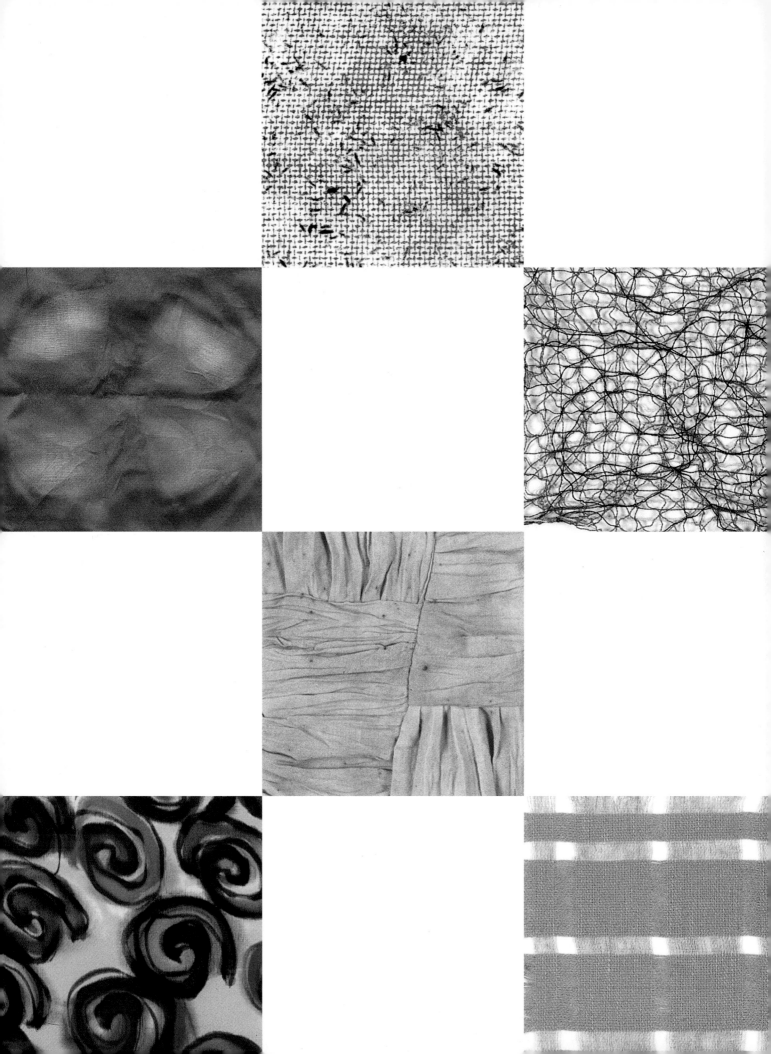

Fabric Recipes

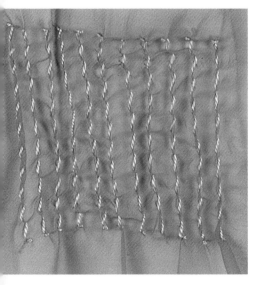

There is intrinsic value in all fabric; even a dime store sale bin could hide a buried treasure. No matter what the fabric looks like, there is a good chance that its appearance and feel can be manipulated into something not only palatable, but breathtaking. A garish print with a beautiful drape can be stripped or bleached to reveal buttery undertones, or at least prepared for a fresh dye job.

Fabric loosens up and becomes remarkably softer when machine-washed, so don't be afraid of the wonderfully patterned piece that seems stiff with little to offer. It is a good idea to run almost every fabric through the washer and dryer, from the dry-clean-only velvets and silks to the more expected cottons. This usually makes the fabric more appealing to work with, and brings the added bonus of being able to wash and dry the finished piece. The wash will remove any sizing that was used in the fabric, making dyeing and painting it easier. Running yardage through the dryer will preshrink it so there will be no worry of a garment or slipcover becoming too small after its first washing. ✦

Layering Fabric

Layering fabric presents a wonderful world of options. The range of material types is seemingly limitless, and combining these only seems to broaden the possibilities.

Torn strips of fabric can have many uses, even costume design; intertwining fabrics can parallel

raw edges of torn fabric add depth and texture

intertwining fine ribbons creates new fabrics

Weaving Torn Strips of Fabric

- Tear the fabric into strips long enough to complete your project. The strips used here are 1 1/2" (4 cm) wide.

- Weave the strips together in the classic under/over pattern of the basket weave. For a dense fabric, keep the edges of the strips butted right up against one another. For a lacier pattern, leave space between them.

- Sew a button on at alternating intersections of two strips. This will secure them from slipping as the garment is worn or laundered.

- To create a soft, frayed edge, run the piece through the washer and dryer.

Ribbon Weaving

- Cut the black and gold ribbon and black edging into strips equal to the length of the project while leaving enough to turn under for the hem and/or seam allowance. Keeping the same criteria in mind, cut the gold edging for the weft of the weaving.

- Weave the ribbons together in a simple basket weave pattern. It may be helpful to pin the loose ends down to a soft surface such as an ironing board.

- On the back side of the weaving, sew all the ribbons into place with small, neat stitches. Make sure the stitches are not visible from the front side.

materials

- green fabric
- purple fabric
- buttons
- thread
- needle
- scissors
- washing machine
- dryer

- black and gold ribbon
- black edging
- gold edging
- black thread
- needle
- scissors

intertwining story lines. Ribbons offer the same design capabilities with the added benefit of already sporting a fine finished edge.

Slashing presents a playful means of displaying multiple fabrics. Try this technique on cloth advent calendars, children's books, or an unusual quilt.

cut openings in fabric to reveal multiple layers

Cutout Patches of Fabric

○ Varying the colors, layer several pieces of fabric on top of one another and sew them all in place in a variety of grid-like patterns. For a slashing design that can be applied to fabric, see the slashing pattern on page 137.

○ Use a small, sharp pair of scissors to puncture a small hole in the middle of an area contained by stitches. Cut through the top layers of fabric in such a way to create tabs of fabric within the defined area. Fold back and iron the cutout patches to reveal the multiple layers of colored fabric.

○ Continue cutting out various patches in this same manner, being careful not to cut through the bottom layer of fabric.

- sewing machine
- pieces of fabric
- thread
- scissors
- iron

strips

A woven piece introduces knotted strips into the design. Torn strip weavings make fun skirts, canopies, or jackets.

ribbons

Informal grosgrain ribbon and upholstery edging come together to form a very refined finished product. Cover headboards or chair backs with a design such as this.

cutouts

Slashing can become quite sculptural as the cut pieces are ironed into place. Use accents like this on shirt or jacket yokes.

crafter's tip

⌂ To avoid a uniform look in slashing projects, do not cut each patch through to the same layer of fabric.

Sheer fabrics are available in a variety of colors, prints, and designs. They work well as overlays backed by thicker fabrics or in screens on their own. Their translucence makes them the ideal palette for many applications.

Decorative stitching presents unlimited design options. Play with colors, threads, and stitches. When adding solid panels, experiment with direction, shape, and size. Incorporate decorative stitches, pleats, and folds for added visual interest. Dye, stitch, and layer a simple solid-color sheer to create the ultimate in daring personalized design.

easily alter the appearance of fabrics

layer fabric over a sheer background to form beautiful panels

Layering Sheer Fabrics

- When selecting fabrics, be careful to consider the purpose of the piece and the desired effect. In this sample, elegant sheer stripes tone down the garish blue color of the bottom material while allowing its wonderful texture to show through.
- Iron the fusible webbing to the back side of the striped fabric and remove its backing paper.
- With both fabrics facing up, place the striped cloth onto the blue material. Iron them so they fuse together. Refer to the manufacturer's label for more complete instructions.
- Treat the new double layer of fabric as one when working it into your project.

Panels of Sheer Material

- If the fabric needs to be joined together, make as narrow a seam as possible.
- Cut the cotton into strips 1/2" (1 cm) wider than the finished width. Fold each edge under by 1/4" (.5 cm).
- Lay the cotton in the striped pattern and pin the pieces in place. Hide seams in the organza with a cotton panel
- From the back side of the fabric, sew the cotton to the organza with small, even stitches down each side of the panels, keeping the stitches close to the edge. Make sure you only capture the portion of the cotton that is turned under.

materials

- blue woven fabric
- sheer striped fabric
- fusible webbing
- iron

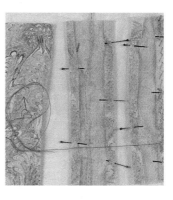

- blue sheer organza
- marbled cotton
- needle
- thread
- scissors
- ruler

trim

Sheers can transform a work fabric into something beautiful. This combination of canvas and sheer trim is great for bustiers and strapless evening gowns that need the support and function of one material and the fashion sense of the other.

simple embellishments with needle and thread

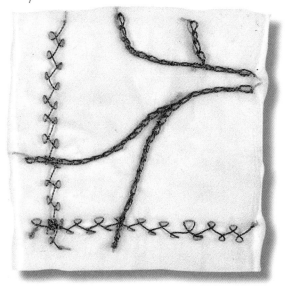

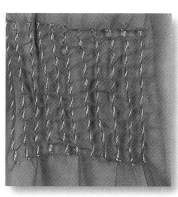

panels

This piece pairs white silk with white organza. The seams were finished with a decorative machine stitch and then the fabrics were pleated. When used in dress or skirt patterns, the panels will reveal themselves in a twist or turn.

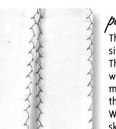

whip stitch

A simple whip stitch not only decorates this blue chiffon but molds it into a new shape. Raised rows are formed by allowing the fabric to gather within the stitch.

Decorative Stitching on Sheers

- Sketch out the design. Lay the white fabric on top of the sketch, and trace the design with the fabric marker.
- This sample displays rows of chain and herringbone stitches (see Recipe Resources for stitching instruction) that play off of the formal feel of the chiffon. Choose a stitch that is attractive from the front and back, as both will be visible when finished.
- Keep knots to the edges of the piece where they will be sewn or glued into the seams of the project, hiding them from view.
- Lightly spray the piece with water to dissolve the fabric marker ink. Let dry.

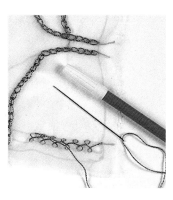

- white chiffon
- blue embroidery thread
- needle
- fabric marker
- scissors
- paper
- pencil
- water

crafter's tip

▲ To make the sheers easier to handle, lightly dust the fabric with spray starch before ironing.

Creating thread fabric simply means turning on a sewing machine. You do not even need to sew in a straight line; all designs work well.

Transforming carded wool into felt is magical. Stitching designs before felting makes the pattern part of the felt instead of surface embellishment.

Crazy lace takes its name from crazy quilts, an assortment of scraps, ribbons, and edging that are more sane than the name implies. Delicate details add a touch of refinement and femininity to bedding, purses, and summer linens.

stitch thread designs to make delicate creations

a new felt piece displaying sewing artistry

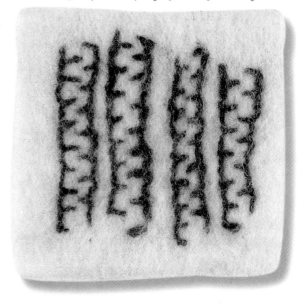

Fabric of Thread

- Cut a piece of soluble stabilizer, available at fabric stores, to the desired size.
- With a sewing machine, create a pattern of stitches over the surface. Though straight stitching is used for this project, free-form, zig-zag, and decorative stitches all work well.
- Change thread and sew a second layer of stitches to secure the stitches of the first. It is important to have many areas of over-lapping stitching; this is how the piece will be held together.
- When all the stitching is completed, soak the piece in water. The webbing will quickly dissolve, leaving only the machine stitches as a self-supporting, supple fabric.

Inlaid Felt Designs

- Make a stack of carded wool, alternating the fiber alignment in each layer. Place the stabilizer on top and secure the pile in the embroidery hoop.
- Stitch the yarn in alternating rows of a buttonhole stitch without knotting the yarn ends. Bring them to the back and cut close to the wool. Remove from hoop.
- Place the piece in a tray of hot, soapy water. The stabilizer will dissolve immediately.
- Knead the wool gently. Scrub more firmly as the fibers mesh and become stronger.
- When the square is tightly meshed, rinse it in cold water and run it through the dryer.

materials

- soluble stabilizer
- sewing machine
- different colored threads
- scissors
- water
- tray

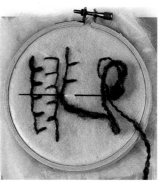

- carded wool
- wool yarn
- soluble stabilizer
- water
- dish soap
- embroidery hoop
- yarn needle
- scissors
- tray
- clothes dryer

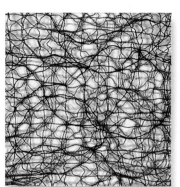

thread

Thread fabrics are so beautiful they could grace everything from a formal dining table to eveningwear. If the time involved in a large project is too daunting, make narrow strips to use as lace edging.

decorative stitching with ribbons and lace

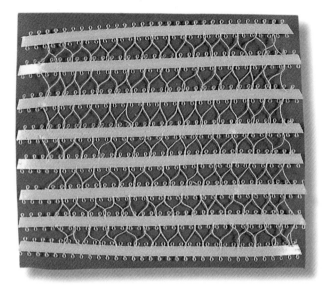

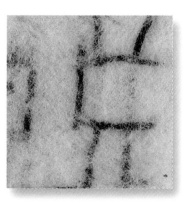

felt

A felted square incorporates blue and white woven carded wool and navy chenille yarn. A thin overlay of white wool was added before the felting process to cloud the overall effect.

Crazy Lace

- On a padded surface such as foam core, lay out strips of ribbon, leaving space between them. Secure the ends of the ribbon by pinning them into the work surface.

- Thread a needle and knot it to the first ribbon. Make a small stitch in the adjacent ribbon, allowing the thread to traverse the space between the two pieces. Continue in a zig-zag pattern along the length of the ribbons. This thread was twisted around itself before making each stitch. Repeat with each row until all the ribbons have been secured to one another.

- Remove the pins and lace fabric from the board.

lace

Create your own nostalgia pieces by incorporating vintage beads and antique laces into your crazy lace designs.

61

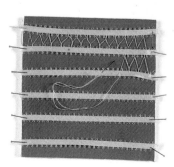

- yellow ribbon
- matching thread
- pins
- foam core
- needle

crafter's tip

To make sure you achieve the desired stitched design, draw your pattern on the soluble stabilizer using a fabric marking pen with ink that will disappear when wet. These useful items are available at any fabric store.

Fabrics drape fluidly along the bias line, which makes shaping curves easy. Preparing bias tubes takes a little time, but it is easy and afterward the work will progress quickly. Experiment with different types of fabrics; even same color designs can be stunning.

Tufting is very traditional in quilts and throws, but think of its possibilities when applied to furnishings, fashion, and home decor. Try various versions of this technique on frames and jackets, or make a super-insulated window covering for the cold winter months.

fabric tubes, cut on the bias, create beautiful arched designs

Layered Curves

∘ Cut the calico fabric into 1 1/4" (3.5 cm) strips along the bias of the fabric. To most easily accomplish this, cut a square of fabric whose straight edges are parallel or perpendicular to the grain line. Fold the square along its diagonal; this is the bias. Cut all the strips parallel to that line. For best results, make sure they are long enough to traverse the required area. Seaming two strips together creates unnecessary bulk.

∘ Iron the edges of the strips under to the wrong side. The width of the fabric tubes should now be 3/8" (.2 cm).

∘ On the right side of the velvet, draw out the pattern of the curved bias tubes. Carefully pin down the tubes, easing the curves into place.

∘ With needle and thread, sew the fabric design into place. From the back side of the velvet, come up through to the top side, just barely catching the edge of the tubing. Go back down through the velvet only. Continue until the entire piece has been sewn.

∘ Iron the fabric to finish.

materials

- blue calico cotton
- blue cotton velvet
- sewing pins
- thread
- needle
- scissors

- iron
- rotary cutter (optional)
- ruler
- ironing board
- fabric marking chalk

anchored batting creates plush finishes

Tufted Fabric with Pearl Beads

- Cut two pieces of fabric 1" (3 cm) larger than the finished size and some batting to match.
- On the front of one piece of fabric, measure off and mark the locations of each tufting point.
- Sandwich the batting between the two fabric pieces, making sure they are right side out.
- With the needle and thread, form a tight stitch at a marked point that pulls the front and back pieces together. Make another stitch that secures the decorative beading to the piece.
- Trim away excess batting from the edges, turn the fabric under along the seam allowances, and slipstitch them together.

- thread
- plaid flannel fabric
- needle
- pearl beads
- quilt batting
- scissors
- fabric marking pen
- ruler

curves

These suede velveteens seldom unravel, so it was unnecessary to turn under the edges, cutting down on the bulk of the piece. Curved designs make fabulous accents to otherwise simple backgrounds.

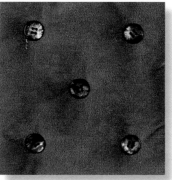

tufting

Buttons add a charming accent to this velvet tufted piece, but there are so many other options to play with. Each tufted point will always have the requisite stitch, but try adding trinkets and charms for a personal touch.

crafter's tip

- For help in placing bias tubes, use fusible webbing or fiber glues. Both are available at fabric stores.

Relying on cloth and batting, stippling transforms fabric into a piece containing depth and pattern. This technique is traditionally used on quilts, but hats, vests, toys, and place mats can all benefit from this application.

Cutwork velvet was often used a few decades ago on what is now treasured vintage clothing. However, buying this type of apparel can be prohibitively expensive, which makes this simple technique an even more appealing option. Turn to lace, wallpaper, and even unfinished puzzles for design inspirations.

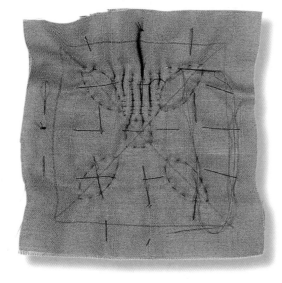

highlight and define a pattern with a series of simple stitches

Stippled Thread Designs

- On the front side of the top piece of fabric, draw the desired stitching design with the fabric marker.

- Sandwich a layer of batting between two squares of fabric. Make sure that the right sides of the material are both facing out. With large stitches, baste the three layers together.

- With a tiny running stitch, outline an open portion of the design, stopping when you have gone three quarters of the way around. Push a small amount of extra batting into the outlined area with the tip of a pencil. Complete the stitching of the perimeter. Proceed on to each area to be treated in the same manner.

- Forming rows of small running stitches, fill in the remaining areas of the design. This sample features two areas that are filled in with rows of stitches that are aligned and two areas where the rows are out of step with one another. See "Experiments in Stippling" section on page 68 for other design ideas.

- Trim away the excess batting from around the edges of the design. Turn the fabric under and slipstitch the sides closed. Remove the basting stitches.

materials

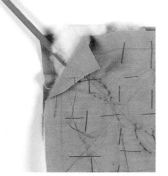

- fabric
- batting
- fabric marker
- needle
- thread
- scissors
- knitting needle

stipple

This stippled piece took its cue from the print of the fabric. The flowers were outlined and stuffed, while the background was filled in with stitches.

fused fabrics form elegant designs

fabric cutwork

Try combining different textures and colors to create personalized cutwork projects such as screens, dresses, lampshades, and robes.

Cutwork Velvet

- Prewash and dry both materials so they are shrunk to their fullest extent.
- Iron the fusible webbing to the back side of the velvet, following the manufacturer's instructions.
- On the back side of the velvet, sketch out your pattern. Remember, the resulting velvet piece will be the mirror image of the drawn design. Cut out the velvet and lay the design on the sheer fabric.
- Remove the backing paper of the fusible webbing and iron the velvet into place.
- It is important to make sure the velvet is firmly secured to the sheer base fabric.

- sheer fabric
- velvet
- fusible webbing
- iron
- scissors
- fabric marker
- washing machine
- dryer

layering fabric

65

crafter's tip

▲ Use a thread of contrasting color when basting. This will make it easier to identify and remove upon completion of the project.

Scale patterns are a classic Victorian accent, but their design applications certainly extend beyond fussy vintage styles. Experiment with different types of fabrics and prints when tackling designs for quilts, toys, and slipcovers.

The wonderful thing about allover stitching is that it can transform the character of a fabric. Layering a structured design over a wild, free-form pattern drastically changes the implications of the pattern. Try using a solid-colored fabric for a truly empty canvas, and combine various types of thread when forming the pattern.

layered rows of triangles form a reptilian design

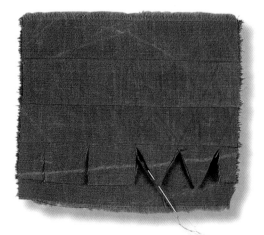 

Scale Pattern

- To make this pattern, follow these directions or refer to the scale pattern supplied on page 136. With the ruler and fabric marker, mark a line on every inch along the fabric's long side.
- Starting at the top, fold the fabric so that the first line meets the second. Sew in place along the line. Repeat with each of the remaining pairs of lines.
- From the front side of the fabric, iron the folds into place. All of them should be pointing downward.
- On every inch of the top fold, clip the fabric perpendicularly to the stitching, being careful not to cut through the line of stitching.

- On the next fold, make the first cut 1/2" (1 cm) from the left side, and from there on clip every 1" (3 cm). The last cut should be 1/2" (1 cm) from the right edge.
- Repeat the last two steps with the remaining folds.
- Push the two corners of a clipped section inside the piece, forming a triangle. With matching thread and a needle, slipstitch the folds in place. Repeat with each remaining clipped section.
- Iron the fabric to crease the folds, and wash it to remove the markings.

materials

- mocha fabric
- sewing machine
- needle
- thread
- scissors
- fabric marker
- iron
- ruler
- washing machine

create new designs with machine stitching

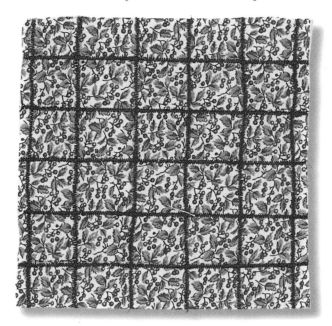

Zig-zag Grid Lines

○ Draw out the pattern of stitching on the right side of the fabric with the fabric marker. As you configure the design, keep in mind the scale of the print versus the stitching pattern and the type of stitch you will be using. This pattern is a simple 1" (3 cm) grid formed with a narrow zig-zag stitch.

○ Carefully sew along the pattern lines with the sewing machine. Take time to adjust the stitch width and length to a proper setting for your design.

○ Trim any loose threads, and wash the fabric to remove any visible markings.

- ■ print fabric
- ■ coordinating thread
- ■ scissors
- ■ fabric marker
- ■ ruler

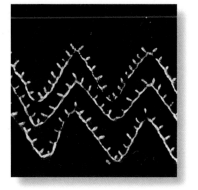

scales

Without needing to be hemmed, the edges of this heavy wool sample are finished with a decorative blanket stitch. At the other end of the spectrum, try using a lightweight cotton to make a delicate bonnet.

scallops

The pattern formed on this solid-colored fabric incorporates two types of machine stitches, lined up in rows. Experiment with novelty threads and various types of cloth.

crafter's tip

⬧ Combine machine stitching with hand stitching for unusual allover stitch designs.

Experiments in Stippling

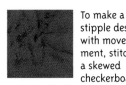 To make a stipple design with movement, stitch a skewed checkerboard pattern. The harlequin design forms fractured waves in the fabric.

 Rows of matched stitches alternate from block to block to form a simple checkerboard pattern. Try experimenting with a multicolored fabric and rows of tiny stitches.

 The random appearance of this swatch was formed by arched rows of stitches. An allover pattern like this is great for stylish hats, or combine this technique with the scale pattern shown on page 66.

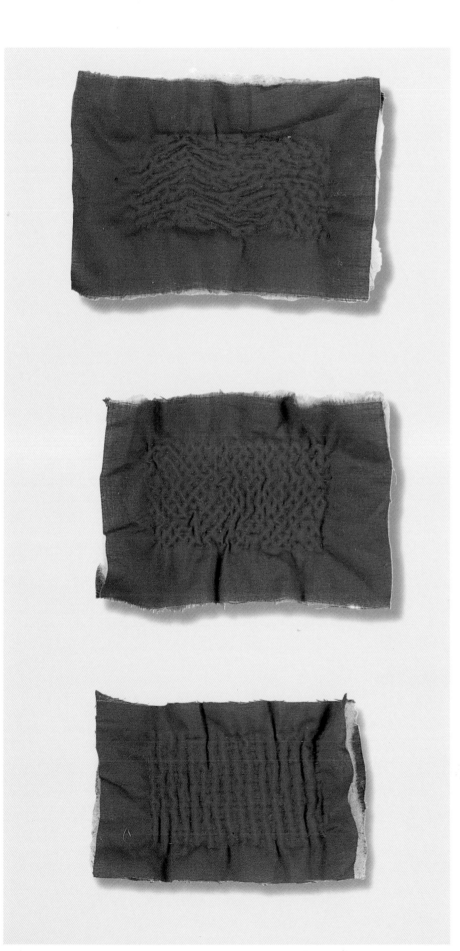

This zig-zag pattern is particularly effective for creating watery backgrounds in quilts, upholstery, and clothing.

To form a subtle, criss-cross pattern, stagger simple running stitches from one row to the next.

Careful placement of stitches that match each vertical row exactly creates the horizontal lines of this swatch. The pin tuck details of this effect are a perfect background for a more abstract design. For diagrams of some of these stipple designs, see page 139.

Manipulating Fabric

While intriguing, burning and branding are not generally considered applicable to most projects. However, when used to alter muslin or calico, branding adds new life. Remember that natural fabrics like cotton, wool, and silk will singe, burn, and char, while synthetic fibers such as polyester, nylon, and acetate melt.

holding fabric to a flame

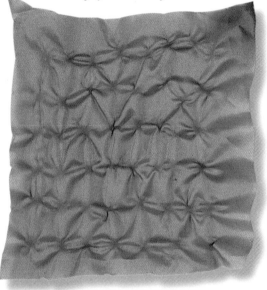

leaving an impression in fabric

Burning Effects

- Work in a well-ventilated area with a ready water supply, such as a sink or garden hose.
- Light a candle to serve as your flame source.
- Hold the area of the fabric you are altering slightly above the flame to melt it and create puckers. If you want a hole in the center of the fabric, hold the piece over the flame and remove it as soon as a hole appears. This looks great if the fabric is layered with an alternate color.
- When you are finished burning your fabric, dunk the piece in a bucket of water to put out smoldering embers.

Branding Images into Fabric

- Shape a piece of wire, and place it on a burner over high heat for several minutes.
- Lay the fabric on a towel near the burner so you may get to it quickly.
- When the "branding iron" is very hot, pick it up off the burner with pliers and quickly place it on the fabric in the chosen spot. Use a potato masher to press the image into the fabric, being careful not to burn through the fabric. Use the pliers to remove the brand from the fabric.
- When you have finished, soak the fabric in water to put out any smoldering embers.

materials

- matches
- candles
- blue nylon fabric
- bucket
- water

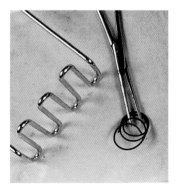

- wire
- needle-nosed pliers or surgical pliers
- stove burner
- towel
- cotton or other non-synthetic fabric
- potato masher
- water

Velvet brings to mind thoughts of luxury. Imprinting a pattern into the soft surface enhances its innate qualities. Look for inspiration at vintage clothing stores; patterned velvets were used with much more frequency in past eras.

creating patterned velvet

burn

A textured red fabric would make a beautiful sheer curtain or room divider that uses back-lighting to show off its subtleties.

brand

The Wild West leaves its mark on this branded and burned cotton fabric. These designs are great for quilting and appliqué.

Embossing Velvet

- Lay the velvet face down over the patterned side of the tile and secure it in place with rubber bands or thumbtacks.
- Lightly spray the back side of the velvet with the starch and press with a hot iron until the pattern of the tile starts to become visible through the back side of the fabric.
- Remove the fabric from the tile. If you are creating an allover pattern, make sure that you do not overlap the design of each pressing. This will create a muddied effect.
- Synthetic velvets produce sharp, crisp designs, while natural fiber velvets will make more subtle patterns.

emboss

A basket weave breakfast tray was used as the pattern for this garnet-colored velvet. Luxurious items such as this are wonderful for everything from dressing gowns to evening gowns.

- printing tile or textured, flat object
- iron
- spray starch
- velvet
- rubber bands

crafter's tip

⬩ Remember when planning your project that burning or branding will sacrifice the structural integrity of the fibers. Practice on a sample first to make sure the piece is suitable for the application you have in mind.

The tiny, irregular pleats in twisted fabric are fun and low maintenance, reminiscent of "hippie" skirts. These pleats applied to silks and satins, however, produce spectacular black tie results.

Pleating techniques like the medieval sample inspire other means of controlling fabric's behavior. Tucks and gathers can be added to further sculpt a material.

A combination of different fabrics can result in a play on the drape of a piece. Incorporate a variety of colors, angles, and pleats in a single item to keep things interesting.

manipulating fabric to unfurl a decorative piece

create a soft, pleated square using two fabrics

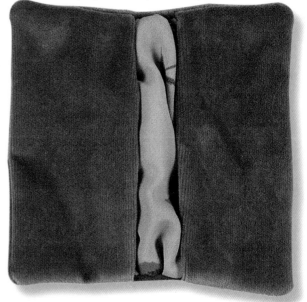

Do the Twist

- Immerse the fabric in water until thoroughly soaked. Remove it and wring it out.
- Hold one end down firmly and twist the other end tightly. When the length of the fabric is tightly twisted and starts to kink up on itself, bring the ends together while holding onto the middle of the strip.
- Keeping the ends together, release the middle point and let the fabric twist back on itself so it resembles a piece of yarn. Slip the joined ends of fabric through the loop in the middle to secure the twisting in place.
- Let the fabric thoroughly dry, then unfurl it.

Medieval Pleats

- Cut two velvet panels and one of rayon into equally sized rectangles.
- Place them side by side with the rayon between the velvets and sew them together along their long edges. Keep a 1/4" (.5 cm) seam allowance.
- Along the rayon's top and bottom edges, run a row of long stitches. Pull the thread tightly to gather the rayon to begin to form a square.
- Fold the velvet over 3/4" (2 cm), hiding the seam of long stitches. Pin in place. Repeat with the other side, and sew the pleats in place.
- To finish the square, back it with some velvet.

materials

- lightweight, natural fiber fabric
- water

- cotton velvet
- rayon print
- sewing machine
- thread
- scissors
- pins
- ruler

spruce up material with a folding technique

twist

Twisted pleats were put together at right angles to skew what might be expected. Larger projects like skirts, curtains, and bedding benefit most from this easy-care look.

bustle

The amount of fabric captured between the two velvet panels inspired further bustling. Additional rows of gathers combined with horizontal stitches create a new royal image. Try this technique on upholstery and home furnishings.

Manipulating Pleats

- Cut a square of fabric three times larger than the finished size.
- Fold the material into pleats as if you were making a paper fan, leaving 3/4" (2 cm) of each fold showing so the fabric looks like clapboard siding. Secure the pleats with pins and iron the fabric.
- On the back side, sew the pleats into place, making sure the stitches will not be seen from the front. Remove the pins.
- Turn the fabric to the front and repeat the last two steps, but this time make the folds perpendicular to the other folds to form fabric squares in the pleats.

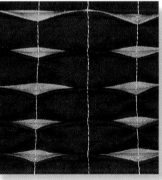

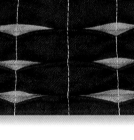

pleat

A striped fabric was pleated in such a way as to obscure one color, which was finally revealed when the pleats were folded back on themselves and stitched in place.

- tie-dyed blue fabric
- iron
- thread
- sewing needle
- pins
- scissors

crafter's tip

Fabric will accept pleats easily when the folds are along or perpendicular to the grain line. Pleats on the bias are more difficult but can be accomplished on lightweight fabrics.

Unlimited patterns can be formed in fabric simply by removing threads. The resulting appearance is one of delicacy as the fabric becomes softer and the surface design more airy. Try re-threading contrasting string back through areas where thread has been removed. Reorienting the fabric so the grain travels on a diagonal will also lend new angles to a piece. Tying off sections of freed warp or weft threads creates a lace-like appearance.

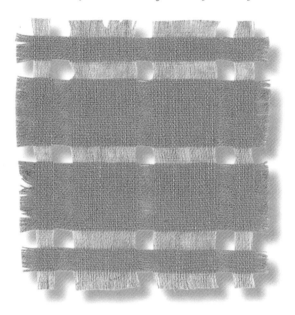

create a new fabric weave by altering the original

designing with knots and thread

Removing Weft and Warp Threads

○ Select a loosely woven fabric constructed of heavyweight threads.

○ Gently tug on one end of the thread you are removing so the fabric becomes gathered along that line. Still pulling on the thread, push the gathers in the opposite direction so they slip off the thread.

○ Continue easing the thread out of the fabric until it is removed. You will notice a gap in the original pattern where this thread used to be. Continue removing threads to create a design.

○ Keep in mind that removing both the warp threads (threads that are vertical) and the weft threads (threads that are horizontal) in an area will result in holes in the fabric.

Tied and Knotted Threads

○ Using the previously described technique, remove a horizontal band of weft threads that measures 1 1/4" (3.5 cm) thick.

○ Thread one of the strands you removed onto a needle, and use this to separate and tie off a grouping of threads in the band created in the fabric. Be sure to keep the stitches neat, and the knots, unless decorative, should be kept on the back side of the fabric. Do not cut off the thread.

○ Travel to the next section of warp threads to be tied off, and knot in the same manner as before. Continue across the band of warp threads.

materials

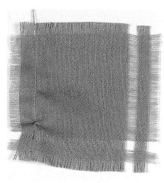

loose-weave fabric

■ loose-weave fabric
■ sewing needle
■ scissors

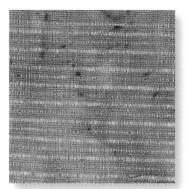

The soft, mottled blue of this fabric is enhanced by the delicate design formed by removing a regular pattern of weft and warp threads. This look is particularly effective when used as accents in fashion design.

give fabric a clever new dimension

Fraying Patches

o Select a warp thread in the middle of the fabric and slip the needle underneath it. Tug gently downward from the top of the material, easing the thread out. A loop will be formed where the needle was inserted into the fabric.

o Continue pulling out warp threads as described until a band has been formed.

o Repeat this process at a lower section of the fabric to create a staggered pattern.

o Iron the loops of thread so they lay neatly, pointing to the bottom edge of the fabric.

o Clip the loops with the scissors to form a neat straight edge of fraying.

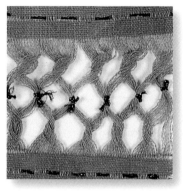

tie

Form lacy patterns by tying off sections of exposed threads. This sample pairs aquamarine material with a metallic purple thread. Apply this technique to the edging of curtains, tablecloths, and other areas of home accessory design.

fray

The casual look of frayed patches can be furthered by altering the direction in which each patch is oriented. Use this playful procedure to accent place mats or children's clothing.

- loose-weave fabric
- large sewing needle
- iron
- scissors

crafter's tip

▲ Some fabrics are made of one color warp thread with a secondary weft color. When threads are removed and manipulated, natural stripes will make themselves evident.

Gathers and puckers set into an otherwise flat piece are intriguing in fashion and home design. Heavyweight upholstery fabrics as well as fine silks will take readily to this technique.

Traditionally used for rugs, joined braids make plush, quilt-like cloth for jackets and hats. Test this simple technique on a wide range of fabrics; you will be surprised at how many outcomes you discover.

Velvet is always luxurious, but watch what happens when it is combined with other fabrics such as silk, lace, or denim.

gather and inset bands of fabric

sew braids together for plush results

Ruching

○ Cut fabric into strips of equal width. The ruched pieces should be three times longer than the others.

○ Set the sewing machine stitch length to its longest setting, and run a row of stitching 1/8" (.25 cm) from the edge on each long side of the longer pieces.

○ Gather the fabric by gently pulling on one of the threads. Repeat with the other row of stitching and for the rest of the long pieces.

○ Adjust the height of the gathered strips to match the shorter strips.

○ Sew the gathered strips to the plain ones, leaving a 1/4" (.5 cm) seam allowance.

Joining Braids

○ Cut the fabric into strips that are 2" (5 cm) wide. You will need three pieces to form each braid.

○ Iron under the raw edges to create a finished width of 1 1/4" (3.5 cm) for each strip.

○ Braid three strips of fabric and sew the ends together to prevent the braid from unraveling. Make as many braids as needed. See the pattern section at the back of the book for additional instructions.

○ With needle and thread, slipstitch the braids together along adjoining sides. Be careful to keep the stitches as hidden from view as possible.

materials

- silver knit fabric
- thread
- scissors
- ruler
- sewing machine

- blue satin
- red satin
- needle
- thread
- scissors
- ruler
- iron

ruched

This delicate, butter yellow silk staggers the ruched panels. Originally vertical, the piece was sewn into a tube and cut apart in a spiral pattern before being put back together.

braiding

Braiding rickrack produces different results from those of the heavier braids in the first sample. The shape of the rickrack interlocks to form an all-over pattern, suitable for cuffs, pockets, collars, or even lampshade trim.

inlaid

Try combining inset and layered pieces for a truly three-dimensional design. Patterns like this make perfect accents for handbags and gloves.

fusible webbing helps to create pieced fabrics

Inlaid Velvet

- Iron the fusible webbing to the back side of the velvet and the faux suede.
- Sketch and cut out assorted shapes from the suede. Arrange them face down on the back side of the velvet.
- Trace the outline of the suede onto the velvet with the fabric marker.
- Carefully cut out tracings, being sure to cut inside the marked lines.
- Remove the backing from the fusible webbing on all pieces of fabric. Arrange them right side up on top of the muslin.
- Iron the piece to adhere the design to the muslin.
- Trim off any excess muslin.

- velvet
- faux suede
- fusible webbing
- fabric marker
- scissors
- iron
- cotton muslin

crafter's tip

⚠ Unexpected combinations are often the most beautiful. Be sure to take the time to play with textures, patterns, and colors.

Felting seems to involve a touch of magic; one minute you have wool, the next, felt! Once you realize you can initiate this process on finished garments, you'll be transforming adult sweaters into child-sized felted jackets in no time.

You may find that stylish rows of bows are the perfect accent for a felted project. They embellish cottons and silks equally well, gracefully moving from casual to eveningwear. Experiment with different bindings, ribbons, and surface textures to see the true range of results.

permanently enmesh wool fibers

castoff knits become something new

Felting

- Separate a thin layer of the batt and lay it in the tray. Place another layer on top, with its fibers perpendicular to those of the first batt. Continue until you have a thick stack.
- Pour in some hot, soapy water. Press down firmly on the wool, and gently knead it with your fingertips.
- As the fibers of the wool start to enmesh, scrub the wool against the bottom of the tray. Add more pressure as the piece can withstand it.
- When the felt is thick and strong, rinse it out in cool water and run it through the dryer.

Recycled Wool Designs

- It is important to make sure the sweater is 100% wool.
- Check the garment carefully, and mend holes and wash out stains according to its instructions.
- Run the sweater through the washing machine three times without drying, using hot water and lots of soap.
- After the third wash, the sweater should have shrunken significantly and the fabric should feel quite thick. You will not be able to discern the individual stitches of the sweater. Run it through the dryer.
- Cut and piece the felt as desired. The edges of the fabric will no longer fray.

materials

- ◼ wool batts
- ◼ water
- ◼ shallow tray
- ◼ dish soap
- ◼ dryer

- ◼ wool sweater
- ◼ laundry soap
- ◼ washing machine

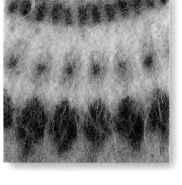

braids

Before this rope was felted, the batts were separated into strips and braided. This will make playful decorations for gift packages and hair ties.

felted

When a sweater is felted, the patterns remain visible. Look to any type of wool garment to try this process, including sweaters, scarves, socks, and mittens.

transform a band of fabric into tidy bows

Rows of Bows

- Cut bands of fabric to the width of the bows.
- Mark a line for every 3" (8 cm) along the longest edges. Gather the fabric at these marks.
- Cut another band 1/4" (.5 cm) wide. Form collars around each gather and sew in place.
- On the background fabric, draw a guideline for the bows. Mark off every 1 1/2" (4 cm).
- Fold one end of the band under to meet the first collared gather. Sew in place and pin to the first mark on the background. Continue in the same manner.
- Sew each gathered point to its corresponding fabric mark.

bows

A bow pattern in brocade is much more elegant than the suede in the first sample. Use this decoration on lingerie, pillows, and jackets.

79

- faux suede
- scissors
- fabric marker
- needle
- thread
- rotary cutter
- ruler
- pins

crafter's tip

▲ Wool batting is wool that has been cleaned and combed so all the fibers are pointing in the same direction. This is available at yarn shops and boutiques.

Without sewing anything, create extraordinary fabric sculpture with the use of stiffeners. Utilizing this simple skill, fancy valances and wall treatments will be made quickly and easily.

Faux fur makes a fantastic blank canvas. Carve out intriguing designs and fun textures, and experiment with different lengths, colors, and types of naps.

Everyone is familiar with the French seams on blue jeans, but new applications are waiting to be discovered. Use French seams to create an overall decorative pattern, or secure their folds with interesting stitching.

create fabric sculptures with strong starches

cutout designs to form new textures and patterns

Stiffening and Shaping

○ Soak the fabric in a fabric stiffener, a thick, milky solution. It is available at most craft and fabric stores. Wring out the excess liquid.

○ Spray a light coat of cooking spray on the mold to ensure easy removal of the dried fabric. Drape the fabric over the mold.

○ With your fingers and a foam brush, work the fabric into the shape of the mold. Take the time to make sure the features are adequately defined. Set aside to dry at least overnight.

○ Gently remove the fabric from the mold, maintaining the intended shape.

Clipping Nap Fabrics

○ Sketch a pattern on paper, keeping in mind the areas that will be cut to different levels and textures.

○ Copy the design onto the fabric, marking the cutting lines with the chalk.

○ Brush the nap so that all the fibers are vertical. Carefully cut away portions of the design, working on small sections at a time. Keep the area you are working on clear of clippings to ensure that the pattern is easy to see.

○ When finished, clean or dust off the chalk as directed on its package.

materials

- fabric stiffener
- mold
- gauze fabric
- foam brush
- cooking spray
- tray

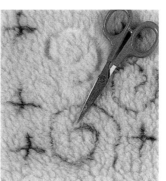

- short nap fabric
- small, sharp scissors
- fabric marking chalk
- pencil
- paper
- brush

double seams expand design possibilities

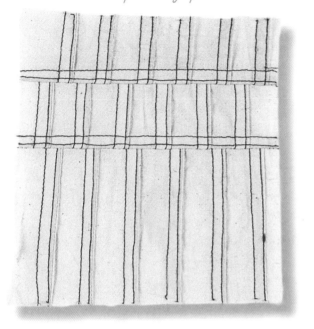

shaping

Ocean waves create a sense of movement, depth, and dimension. Remember that the thinner the fabric, the more detail you will be able to capture.

clipping

Faux furs come in a wide selection of styles, colors, and patterns. Clip the naps into new designs to add interesting textures.

double seams

A burglar lurks behind these uneven French seams. Beads and ribbons could be encased in the folds to make fine eveningwear or playful decorations.

French Seam Detailing

- Place two pieces of fabric right sides together. Sew a line of straight stitches with a 1/4" (.5 cm) seam allowance.
- Turn the pieces of fabric over the seam so their back sides are together. Iron the fold.
- Sew another 3/8" (.2 cm) seam along the folded seam edge. This will encase the raw edges and obscure them from view.
- Fold the tab you created down flat. Run a row of stitches as close to the edge as possible to secure it in place.
- This sample displays rows of French seams cut apart horizontally and sewn together in a staggered fashion.

- cotton muslin
- red thread
- scissors
- sewing machine
- iron
- ruler

crafter's tip

⌂ If fabric stiffeners are not readily available, papier-mâché or wallpaper paste will work just as well.

Rug hooking needn't be limited to rugs; its beauty definitely qualifies it as fine art. In addition to making framed hookings for your walls, try recycling lightweight fabrics into hooked pieces for clothing, book covers, and runners.

Many artists find that a mirror is a powerful design tool and will use one to check that their design looks right.

Elastic thread puckers, gathers, and pulls fabric into intriguing new configurations. Add this type of detailing to blouses, waistbands, and pillowcases.

lush designs formed with strips of wool and a hook

generate complex designs with a mirror

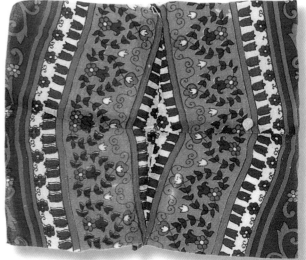

Rug Hooking

- Draw the pattern onto the burlap. Keep the image at least 1 1/2" (4 cm) from the edges.
- Insert the hook into the burlap. From the back, pull the tail of one wool strip 1/8" (.25 cm) to 1/4" (.5 cm) above the surface.
- Continue, keeping each loop a uniform height and as close to the previous one as possible. Maintain a steady tension on the burlap.
- At the end of a strip, pull the tail up to the front side and cut to the right height.
- When finished, sew the rug tape close to the hooked edges and turn under.

Kaleidoscope Patterns

- Start with a piece of fabric much larger than the finished size of the project. To accomplish the mirrored look, you will need lengths of repeating patterns from which to pick and choose the required motifs.
- Select a portion of the design that appeals to you. Hold the mirror perpendicular to the fabric and move it over the material until you see a pattern you like.
- Cut out two areas of the section you chose, and sew them together as seen through the mirror. Be sure to pay attention to angles.
- Repeat until the design has reached the intended complexity.

 materials

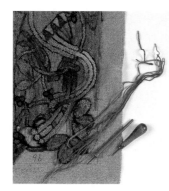

- rug hook or small crochet hook
- wool flannel cut into 1/8" (.25 cm) strips
- burlap
- scissors
- thread
- needle
- rug tape
- indelible marker
- ruler

- print fabric
- thread
- sewing machine
- scissors
- small mirror

hooked

This sample shows the abstract side of traditional rug hooking and plays with color and shading. Do not be limited by the expectations of this technique; experiment with content and form.

multiple gathers provide added texture

mirror

Make a fractured design using a kaleidoscope patchwork of marbled fabrics. A larger piece of this sample would show that the pattern forms a complete circle.

Stitching with Elastic Thread

○ Wind the bobbin with elastic thread, keeping the tension only modestly snug. Use regular sewing thread for the top thread.

○ Draw out a pattern of stitching on the fabric. Remember that once sewn, the fabric will measure a good deal smaller than its starting dimensions. Start on some scrap material so you can see the effect of different stitch patterns.

○ With the sewing machine set at a medium-length stitch, sew along design lines as normal. As you sew, the fabric will gather up. Be careful to prevent jamming.

elastic

Luxurious silks have more areas that reflect light when puckered by elastic thread. At the other end of the spectrum, try this application on upholstery-weight fabrics.

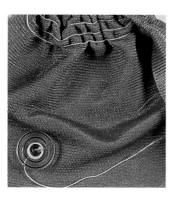

- fabric
- sewing machine
- elastic thread
- thread
- scissors
- fabric marker
- scrap material

crafter's tip

▲ To escape old concepts about color, put a bunch of colored paint chips in a bowl and keep mixing up the batch. Make note every time you see a color combination you like.

Experiments in Removing Warp and Weft

 This elegant fabric rendition was created by simply removing a series of warp threads. Carefully count out the threads to ensure a visually repetitive pattern.

 In fabrics such as this one, the removal of the weft threads creates a much more subtle striping. Experiment with small swatches of the materials to test their personal characteristics.

 Grids can be created in all scales. Where both weft and warp threads have been removed, holes appear in the fabric. Regular patterns are perfectly suited for covering projects such as books and boxes.

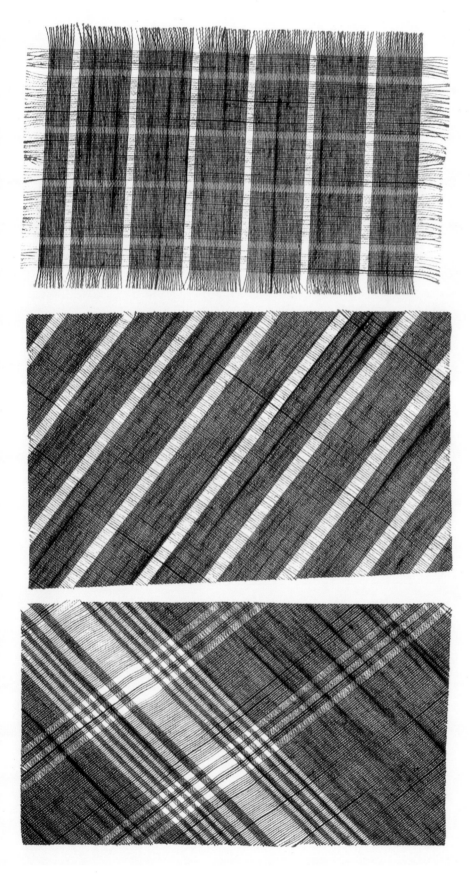

Remove numerous threads from both warp and weft to dramatically change the nature of a fabric. This not only creates a lacier pattern, but it thins the material for a much more fluid drape.

By cutting out the fabric on the bias, diagonal stripes are created. Check the pattern to see if this option will work for your project. Dresses, skirts, and scarves are well suited for this layout.

This piece was cut on the bias as well, allowing the diagonal plaid accent. Try layering these fabrics over a base of a different color.

Fabric Surface Finishes

Variations on the basic marbling technique are seemingly endless. The plaid pattern created in the project is an example of a masking technique that can be expanded on and further manipulated to form even more wonderful designs. Test the technique on a multicolored fabric, or create a more intricate folded pattern in the fabric to discover endless possible displays.

sewn areas divide a marble pattern

Plaid Marbling

- Prewash and dry the fabric. Prepare the alum as directed on the package. Soak the fabric in the alum solution and dry. Measure and mark off the lines that define the plaid.

- Fold the area to be kept white along the middle of its width. Machine-stitch the fold in place. Repeat with each other area that is to be kept clear of the inks.

- Prepare the methyl cellulose bath as directed by the manufacturer.

- Apply the inks to the surface of the bath with quick movements. Style the inks into the desired design with the rakes, combs, and/or stylus. This sample features a bouquet pattern.

- Gently lay the fabric face down onto the inks in one smooth motion. Let it sit for just a moment and then remove it from the bath. Be careful not to get ink on the masked sections.

- Begin rinsing the fabric by pouring water over just the front of it to remove excess inks. Immerse the fabric in a bucket of clean water to finish the rinse.

- Hang up the fabric and allow it to dry thoroughly before removing the stitching.

- Spread out the fabric and iron it well to remove the creases and aid in the heat setting. Complete the heat setting by running the piece through the dryer for an hour.

materials

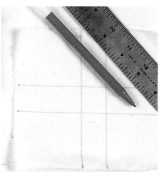

- methyl cellulose
- clear ammonia (for the methyl cellulose bath)
- water
- bucket
- marbling acrylics
- combs, rakes, stylus
- cotton fabric
- alum

- iron
- ruler
- fabric marker
- sewing machine
- thread
- scissors
- washing machine
- dryer

The vibrant colors of painted silk make this an enticing medium to work in. The setting of the colors is what transforms the dull painted silk into a piece rich with color and luminescence. The choice of dye will affect the method required to set the colors, so for the beginner, look for one that can be set easily, without the use of large and expensive commercial equipment.

hand-painted inventions with luminescence

Silk Painting

- Prewash the silk to remove any sizing.
- Pull the silk taut over a canvas stretcher frame that is slightly larger than the fabric. Secure with the silk tacks.
- Working from the lightest color to the darkest, start painting out the design with broad, flat strokes. Wait for each color to dry, five to twenty minutes as needed, before adding the next. Allow the piece to dry thoroughly before moving.
- Different types of dyes have various heat setting requirements. This dye, from the liquid procion H series, was set in a vertical steamer. Refer to the dye manufacturer's instructions for setting the colors properly.

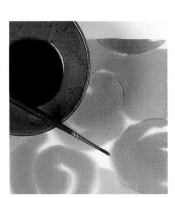

- silk crepe de chine
- assortment of silk dyes, mixed following the manufacturer's directions
- watercolor brushes
- canvas stretcher frame
- silk tacks
- washing machine
- color setting equipment as listed by dye manufacturer

marble
The marbling process can be adjusted infinitely. This piece, the result of marbling with a very thick, hot bath, exhibits muted, blended tones.

dye
The same design, in a smaller scale, in more vibrant hues, can create surprisingly varied results.

crafter's tip

▲ Iron patterns cut from freezer wrap onto fabric act as a mask against marbling inks. Once the fabric has been thoroughly rinsed, remove the freezer paper by carefully peeling it from the surface.

Batik rarely gets to shine as an allover design, but these samples make wonderful mottled surfaces for garments, upholstery, and even jewelry.

With very little effort, rubbed fabrics can become intricately designed masterpieces. Look to bulk food bins and the seashore for pattern ideas that will deftly enhance clutch purses, cummerbunds, and ties.

Clamping is a sure way to leave your mark. Try fashioning monogram and signature forms out of wood or Plexiglas for a personal imprint on towels, bed linens, and cloth napkins.

put wax resistance to work

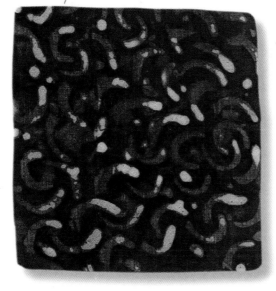

easily imprint textures onto fabric

Batik Patterns

○ Melt the wax as directed in "Objects in Wax" on page 118. Wax is hot enough when it can be easily brushed over the surface and quickly absorbed by a piece of fabric.

○ Working quickly, brush the wax over the material in the desired pattern. Where there is wax, there will be no color. Let the wax cool.

○ Immerse the fabric in a dye bath. Let it sit until it is slightly darker than the desired color. Remove it and rinse.

○ Place the fabric between two layers of scrap cloth. Press with a hot iron until all the wax has been absorbed by the scraps.

Rubbed Fabrics

○ Spray the adhesive over the chipboard and affix the pattern. For this sample, two boards were used: one features rice, the other features needlepoint canvas.

○ Dab the paint over the textured surface with the T-shirt fabric and very carefully lay the fabric in place, face down.

○ Place a sheet of wax paper over the fabric. Quickly and firmly roll the rolling pin once over the stack. Remove the fabric, being careful not to smudge the image.

○ Repeat as necessary to achieve the desired layers of color. Be sure to let each color application set for several minutes before adding the next.

materials

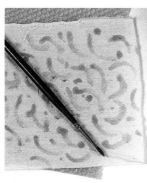

- beeswax
- paintbrush
- stove
- cooking pot
- tin can
- cotton muslin
- tin foil
- iron
- scrap fabric
- fabric dyes
- water
- bucket

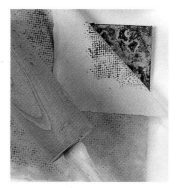

- chipboard
- textured item
- spray adhesive
- oil paints
- wax paper
- rolling pin
- wadded T-shirt material
- fabric

batik

After the fabric was dyed yellow, more wax was added and the fabric was repeatedly crumpled. The piece was then dyed green and the wax was removed as usual. The result is a two-color, crackled effect.

blocking out dyes with forms and pressure

imprint

This prequilted fabric was imprinted twice with the rice board in two different colors. Originally white, the fabric was dyed purple to enhance the rubbed image.

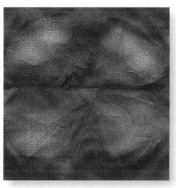

Clamping and Dyeing

- For each clamped area two waterproof forms are needed. The ones used here were cut from luon, a type of thin wood.
- Screw the clamps down very tightly to fix the forms in place on the fabric. The area where the forms are will not accept the dye.
- Mix the dye bath as directed on its package.
- Immerse the clamped fabric in the dye. Once the color is slightly darker than what you want, remove the piece and rinse thoroughly.
- Allow the fabric to dry before removing the clamps.

clamp

Felts, cottons, and satins all work well with the clamping and dyeing technique. Experiment with scraps before committing to a large project.

89

- waterproof forms
- C clamps
- bucket
- dyes
- cotton/lycra
- water

crafter's tip

 When preparing a dye bath for clamping, make sure that the container is large enough to accept the clamps.

Treasured fine art photos take on new life when displayed on an unexpected medium. Try overlapping or mirroring images, or cut a photograph into pieces before arranging it on the material.

The type of fabric used will affect a piece's finished look. Keep in mind the feel you are trying to convey as you choose your materials.

Photo transfers offer varied means of expression. Choose the technique that suits you and your project best. Photo emulsions produce a more subdued color palette than photo transfers do.

attaching emulsions to fabric

Photo Emulsions

- Take a slide of your chosen image to a photographer or photo printing store and have them make a print of it using Polaroid film type 669, 59, 559, or 809. This is different from the standard Polaroid instant camera film you may have at home.

- Set up your equipment near the stove, using items that you will never eat from. Prepare a pan of cold water and bring a pot of water to a boil. You should be wearing gloves to protect your hands during this process.

- Submerge the photo in the pot and simmer it for three or four minutes. Use a pair of tongs to remove the photograph and immediately place it in the pan of cold water.

- While the photograph is in the water, use your gloved finger-tips to gently push the image from the edges of the print to remove it from the backing of the photograph.

- Once the backing has been removed, only the emulsion should be floating in the water. Carefully remove it and place it on your fabric. Be sure to smooth out air bubbles and excess water. The emulsion can be manipulated to fold over itself, stretch, tear, etc., to suit your design needs.

- Hang the fabric up to dry, weighting down the bottom with clothespins to ensure that the fabric dries straight.

materials

- color print
- tight-fitting rubber gloves
- shallow pan
- cooking pot
- water
- metal tongs
- fabric
- stove
- clothespins

transferring photocopies to cloth

emulsion

Tea was poured onto the front and back of this completed photo emulsion to enhance the color of the pears and create a patina.

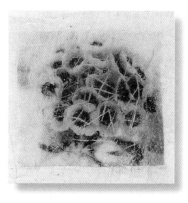

transfer

An acrylic transfer of anemones takes on a rugged, earthy feel when placed on a nubbly cotton gauze. The image was then sliced with a razor blade and stretched to further fracture its lines.

Photos to Fabric

○ Select a picture to be transferred to fabric and make a color photocopy of it. Keep in mind that the finished image will be a mirrored version of the original. Carefully cut out the portion of the photocopy to be transferred.

○ Place the photocopy face up on a sheet of wax paper and brush a generous coat of the fabric transfer medium over it. Carefully lift the image off the wax paper and place it face down on the white fabric. Press down firmly.

○ Allow the medium to dry thoroughly. Soak the fabric in water and gently rub off the paper. Cut out the portions of the image to be used and adhere them to the green fabric using the fabric transfer medium as glue.

crafter's tips

▲ An easy way to remove a photo emulsion from a cold water bath is to slip a piece of wax paper beneath it. Hold two corners of the emulsion in place and use the motion of the water to adjust the image as you want it to appear on the finished piece.

▲ Wet the fabric before you place an emulsion on it. This will make it easier to adjust the image after it has been transferred.

▲ To quickly transfer a photograph to fabric, take your image to a photocopy shop that can put the picture onto heat transfer paper. When you get home, all you have to do is iron the photo into place.

- fabric transfer medium
- color photocopy of a photograph
- paintbrush
- wax paper
- water
- white fabric
- green fabric
- scissors
- tray

Nature offers unending inspiration for life, work, and art. Prints of leaves are perfect accents for holiday harvest napkins or spring place settings. Sand, on the other hand, makes a much more subtle mark. Muted tones blend into one another with fractured outlines on leggings and scarves.

Gocco printing is a quick and easy way of silk screening projects without a lot of hassle. For the craftsperson who needs to make multiple prints of the same design, this technique will provide quick results, with a fairly minimal investment in a Gocco machine.

nature leaves its mark

soft patterns are masked out with sand

Nature Prints

○ Cover the work surface with some clean scrap paper. Lay the fabric you are decorating on top of this.

○ Arrange the leaves over the fabric in a pattern you find appealing.

○ Place a sheet of tracing paper on top of the leaves, and hammer the entire surface thoroughly to release the natural dyes of the foliage onto the fabric. The tracing paper will allow you to see where to hammer while protecting the tool from the pigments.

○ Remove the fabric from between the tracing paper and scrap paper, and discard the papers.

Sand Painting

○ Lay the fabric out on a protected flat surface. Pour a thin layer of sand over the entire surface of the fabric.

○ With the hair dryer, blow a pattern into the sand. This will expose certain portions of the fabric.

○ Mist the fabric lightly with a strong color. Blow-dry the sand and rearrange it to reveal different areas of the fabric. Add a second color in the same manner as before. Repeat for as many other colors as needed.

○ Let the piece dry completely before brushing off the sand.

○ Rinse out the fabric and heat-set the colors.

materials

- assorted leaves
- scrap paper
- hammer
- fabric
- tracing paper
- protected flat surface

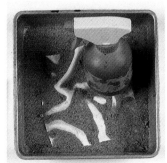

- fine sand
- hair dryer
- knit fabric
- spray bottle
- strong fabric pigments such as concentrated dyes or marbling acrylics
- protected flat surface
- water

*a simple silk screening technique
that creates professional prints*

nature

Leaf prints age into a range of beautiful brown hues. While wonderful as accents, these images are also suitable for allover designs.

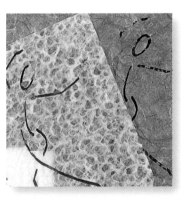

sand

This pale blue silk was layered with dark green and black inks, using the sand as a mask. Once dry, hand-drawn silver lines were added.

Gocco Printing

○ Sketch out the desired design on paper. Keep in mind the scope and scale of the finished project.

○ Following the manufacturer's directions, expose the drawing onto a sensitized screen in the Gocco machine with flash bulbs.

○ Lift the acetate top from the screen. Squeeze inks onto the design on the screen before lowering the acetate back into place.

○ As directed, insert the screen into the top portion of the Gocco machine and carefully line up the fabric underneath. Press the top of the Gocco machine to the fabric firmly. Repeat the process as necessary to create the overall pattern.

○ Each screen will produce approximately fifty prints.

Gocco

Textured fabrics make an image even more unique and unusual. Experiment with nubby silks, soft sheers, and busy tapestries.

■ Gocco machine by Riso Kagaku Corp., available at art supply stores

■ high-mesh silk screening inks

■ paper

■ marker

■ fabric

crafter's tip

▲ Fresh flowers are fine to imprint on paper but tend to be too wet to leave a distinct likeness on cloth. If you are trying to set a floral image onto fabric, let the flower dry out partially first.

othing could be easier than these three ways to embellish your fabrics. Stencilling and block printing allow the application of complicated patterns to move along at a steady clip. Once the block or stencil is prepared, the repetitive nature of the process makes for quick progress.

Rubber stamping is a great alternative if your sketching skills are not what you wish them to be. With the growth of the rubber stamping industry, there are now thousands of available pictures that span a spectrum of topics.

stippled brush strokes fill in a predetermined pattern

carve and print unique repetitive patterns

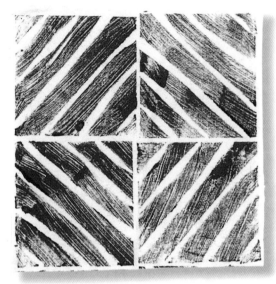

Stencilling

- Sketch out your pattern on heavy white paper. Cut out and remove the portions of the design that are to be colored in with the paint.
- Protect the work surface with newspaper, and lay the design on top of the fabric.
- Tap the brush repeatedly into a small pool of paint, working the color up into the bristles. Do not overfill the brush with paint.
- Gently dab the brush over the stencil and fabric, filling in the exposed areas of fabric thoroughly.
- Remove the stencil and allow the image to dry before adding additional decoration.

Block Printing

- Prepare the fabric by making sure that it is ironed flat and laid out on some newspaper to protect the work surface.
- Sketch the pattern on the foam core and cut out the portions that you do not want to be inked.
- Brush the paint over the surface of the foam core to create striations in the color.
- Very firmly, press the block of foam onto the fabric, ink side down. Repeat as necessary. For this sample, the block was rotated forty-five degrees each time it was stamped.

materials

- gray fabric
- black fabric paint
- stipple paintbrush
- newspapers
- pencil
- heavy white paper
- craft knife

- foam core
- craft knife
- foam brush
- fabric paints
- white fabric
- pencil
- iron
- newspaper

professional designs add instant appeal

Rubber Stamping

- To make a stamp pad, fold some scrap fabric into a firm, neat square and soak it with ink. If you are working with multiple colors, it is best to start with the lightest color and finish with the darkest.

- Before changing colors, clean the stamp off as much as possible by repeatedly pressing it on a scrap of paper.

- This piece features two different stamped images in black ink, on a multicolored background fabric.

- When you are finished, make sure that the rubber stamp is clean before storing it for future use.

- fabric inks
- rubber stamp
- fabric
- absorbent scrap fabric
- scrap paper

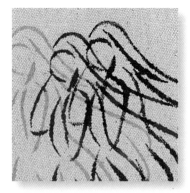

stencil

Try combining colors and overlapping images to create one-of-a-kind accents for children's clothing and home accessories.

block print

An abstract figure dances across the fabric without a care, thanks to the simplicity of the technique. Large surfaces can be covered quickly, making this a great application for quilts, coats, and slipcovers.

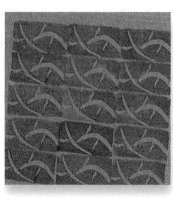

rubber stamp

In contrast to the random pattern of the project, a simple brick stamp was repeatedly pressed onto the fabric in a very strict design.

crafter's tip

▲ Instead of foam core, try carving your block prints from rubber erasers or linoleum.

Coffee stains generally tend to be feared, but try looking at these accidents from another angle. A fabric that you thought was ruined by a coffee spill may actually have been given a vintage charm. Tea-dyeing can produce a wonderful variety of colors and results as well.

Beneath the seemingly mundane surface of a solid-color fabric can lie surprises. Applying bleach to sections of the cloth can result in new color combinations and reveal unexpected base hues.

percolating rich dye colors

herbal dyes create natural hues

Antiquing with Coffee

- Make a pot of coffee to use as dye. The stronger the coffee, the more color it will leave on the fabric.
- To create an allover wash of color, submerge the material in hot coffee and let sit until it reaches a shade slightly darker than the desired color.
- If a more mottled look is in order, lay the fabric in front of you and gently dab patches of coffee onto it with a piece of cotton fabric. Continue in a manner that suggests the uneven aging of fabric if left in the sun.
- Repeat until the coffee stains reach the desired intensity.

Dyeing with Teas

- Prewash and dry your fabric, and treat it with an alum mordant to ensure a strong color result.
- Make several pots of tea a bit stronger than usual, until you have enough to fill a large plastic bucket at least halfway.
- Submerge the fabric in the tea and allow it to sit until it has reached the desired color. Stir occasionally to ensure an even absorption of the dye.
- Remove the fabric from the bucket and rinse it thoroughly. Heat-set the color by running the piece through the dryer.

materials

- coffee
- cotton fabric
- bucket
- cotton

- gauze fabric
- alum
- herbal tea
- bucket
- washing machine
- dryer
- water
- large spoon

coffee
Silk brocade is a wonderful candidate to accept the rich tones of coffee. Upholstery-weight cotton canvas also provides lush hues.

tea
To color this lightweight cotton, a berry-based tea was used. The fabric was then twisted to form the pleats.

remove dye to expand the range of colors

Bleaching to Form Gradations

- Apply bleach with a paintbrush, using a ruler as a guide. Squirt bottles, calligraphy ink pens, and eyedroppers may also be used.
- To temper the strength of the bleach, dilute it with a bit of water.
- Allow the bleach to sit on the fabric until the new color reaches the desired intensity, then rinse immediately in water.
- Natural fiber fabrics react better to this treatment than synthetics, but there are always exceptions. Try a test swatch of any cloth before beginning a large project.

bleach
A piece that began as pale blue denim was dyed an even deeper shade of blue. The color was then removed down to white by applying bleach with a small paintbrush.

- colored fabric
- paintbrush
- bleach
- water

crafter's tip
⚠ When dyeing with teas, you will find that pretreating the fabric with a mordant will produce results that range from a deep, rich tone to a completely unexpected different color.

Wallpaper paste has much more potential than originally intended; it carries color and is the surface in which a pattern is carved. Use these wallpaper paste ideas to decorate chair backs, trunk covers, and place mats.

Salty winter sidewalks were the inspiration for the freezing and salting technique. The watery tones are formed by droplets of color that work their way through the small holes made in the ice by the salt. Use paints, marbling acrylics, or dyes to color the fabric in a concentration strong enough to stand up to the diluting effects of the melting ice.

Unusual crumpled and dyed fabrics make beautiful skirts, jackets, and sheets. Experiment with different types of fabrics and colors.

carve out designs on fabric

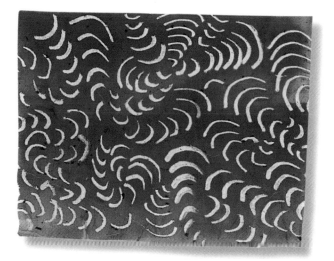

ice formations form the groundwork for designs

Wallpaper Paste Fabrics

- Keep in mind this creates a very stiff result that is not suitable for clothing.
- Spread the muslin out on a protected work surface. Brush a generous coat of paste evenly over the surface and let it sit to dry overnight.
- Brush the color over the paste. In a moment or so, the paste will absorb the color and become wet again.
- Scrape away portions of the paste with a chopstick. Beneath the paste, you will find that the fabric is still white.
- Let the colored paste dry before using the fabric.

Freezing and Salting

- Weight the fabric to the bottom of a shallow pan with pennies. Make sure it lays flat.
- Cover the piece with 1/4" (.5 cm) of water, and place the pan on a level surface in the freezer.
- Once the water has frozen, sprinkle a small handful of salt over the surface.
- As the ice melts, a rutted pattern will form where the salt has hit it. At this point, brush the color over the entire surface of the ice. Wipe off any excess dye. Let the ice melt while occasionally pouring off the water.
- Refreeze and salt for each color.

materials

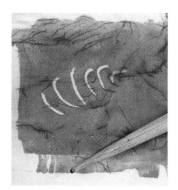

- wallpaper paste
- foam brush
- muslin
- chopstick
- fabric dyes

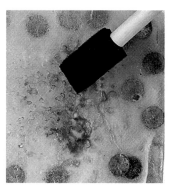

- shallow pan
- freezer
- strong colors for fabrics
- sea salt
- pennies
- foam brush
- rag
- fabric
- water

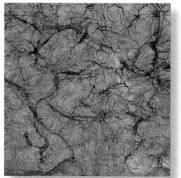

paste

This wallpaper paste-treated muslin was repeatedly crinkled before being painted with a blue dye. The cracks in the paste caused by the crumpling process accept the color of the dye much more strongly than where the paste is intact.

the drying fabric's shape affects the dye pattern

ice patterns

Soften hardy canvas with the fluid patterns of colored melting ice. Different fabrics absorb moisture in varying intensities, so be sure to test the fabric for the range of possibilities.

Dyeing and Crumpling

- Mix the dye as directed on its package in a container large enough to accept your fabric.
- Dip the fabric into the dye and let it sit for just a few minutes, but do not allow the color to get too dark. If this does occur, further treatment of the fabric will not show up.
- Remove the fabric from the dye and wad it up into a tight ball. Secure the configuration with rubber bands and set aside to dry.
- Once dry, unfurl the fabric and press flat.

twisted

Instead of being crumpled, this beautiful fabric was formed by twisting/pleating it immediately after it was removed from the dye bath.

- lightweight lining material
- fabric dye
- rubber bands
- container
- iron

crafter's tip

For wallpaper paste projects, the lighter the coat of paste, the less stiff the final piece will be.

Inexpensive and lightweight, ceiling plugs are an excellent choice for the wrapping technique. Create curtains, lampshades, or baskets, and include beads or ribbons in the design. Experiment with wrap configuration and disk size. Anything that is fairly stiff with a hole in its center will work well.

Constructing on fabric provides an opportunity to include nontraditional elements in fiber design. The expanded range of acceptable additions allows for unexpected uses for the finished pieces. Try designing cards and table tiles to be put under glass.

wrapped disks form unusual accents

Fabric-Wrapped Disks

○ It is important to remember that the disks will not be removed from the finished piece. Therefore, this is not an appropriate technique for clothing. Please note that for clarity, the how-to photos feature a different colored yarn for each step.

○ Wrap a 1/4" (.5 cm) band of chenille around the diameter of a ceiling plug. Form another 1/4" (.5 cm) band that crosses the first.

○ Keeping the chenille inside the legs of the "x," form two parallel lines from top to bottom. Each should be butted up against the "x." Repeat the formation in the other direction.

○ Continue making pairs of parallel lines, alternating top to bottom and left to right, until the disk is completely wrapped. Bring the chenille to the back side of the disk.

○ Cut the chenille, leaving an 8" (20 cm) tail. With the tapestry needle, thread it up through the center of the disk and then back down, being sure to capture several of the wraps. Tie a knot to secure the wrapping. Trim the excess yarn.

○ Make as many disks as desired and sew them together with needle and thread.

materials

▪ cotton chenille

▪ ceiling plugs or washers

▪ tapestry needle

▪ scissors

▪ sewing needle

▪ thread

▪ ruler

three-dimensional collages create a new surface

Fabric Constructions

- Collect an assortment of items and arrange them until a pleasing pattern is formed. Be sure that the pieces are appropriate for the intended use of the finished product.
- Choose a background fabric, taking color, texture, and fiber content into account. This muslin was tea-dyed and painted.
- Lightly sketch out the design onto the fabric. Starting with the background items, glue each piece to the material. Let dry.
- If the project will be used as wearable art, sew the items to the fabric instead.
- To remove the pen markings, gently dab them with a damp sponge.

- cotton muslin fabric
- tea
- watercolors
- paintbrushes
- PVA glue
- assorted items
- fabric marker
- sponge
- water

wrap

Heavy washers at the base of larger circles give this piece potential to become a floor mat or hot plate. The disks were formed in the same manner as the project, but two alternating colors were used instead of one.

collage

Metallic gold and mottled French wire ribbons make this variation seem more refined than its earth-toned counterpart. Experiment with buttons, sea shells, and beads for fabrics to be used on valances, banners, and signs.

crafter's tip

▲ Hardware stores are the best resource for finding ceiling plugs and washers for a wrapping project.

Experiments in Tea-dyeing

 Mordant-treated fabric was allowed to dry while crumpled before being dyed with a lemon tea. This caused streaks of concentrated areas of alum that produced purplish striations.

 Chamomile and mint tea applied to alumed fabric produced a golden hue with a hint of green.

 Chamomile tea has a mild effect on regular cloth, but the fabric takes on a warm buttery tone when treated with mordant.

 Though this sample is alumed cotton dyed with coffee, you can achieve a similar, intense tea color by strengthening the tea brew.

lemon tea on alumed cotton

chamomile and mint tea on alumed cotton

chamomile tea on alumed cotton

strong tea or coffee on alumed cotton

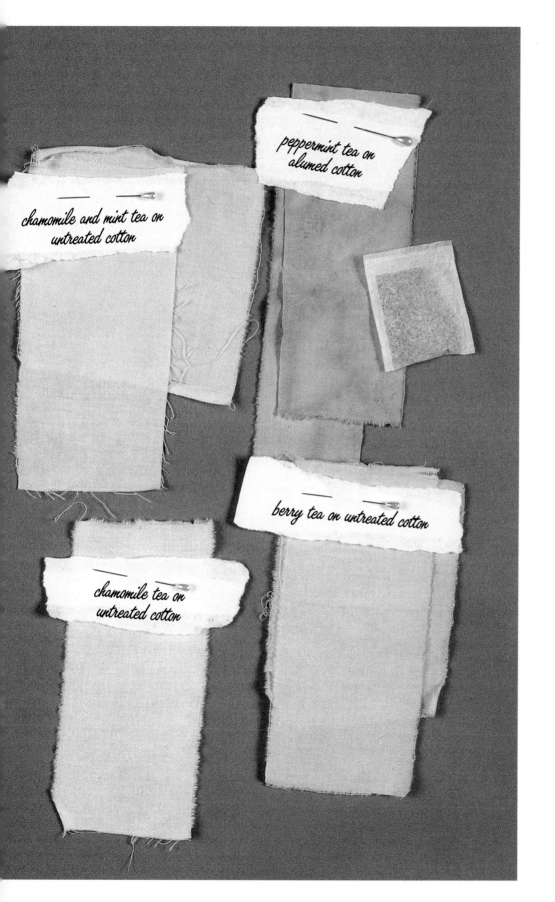

chamomile and mint tea on
untreated cotton

peppermint tea on
alumed cotton

berry tea on untreated cotton

chamomile tea on
untreated cotton

This swatch shows the same chamomile and mint tea's effect on untreated cotton.

A peppermint-based tea dye is affected differently by various fabric treatments. The plain fabric took on a soft, pale yellow tone, while this alumed piece became a drab olive green.

Sometimes only slight differences will appear on mordanted and unmordanted fabric swatches. This chamomile tea produces a paler color in an untreated swatch. Keep in mind that different mordants can have divergent effects.

A soft tone results from the coloring of a berry-based tea.

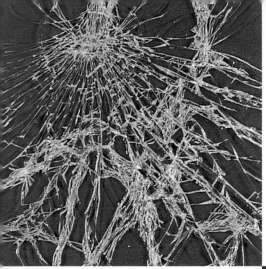

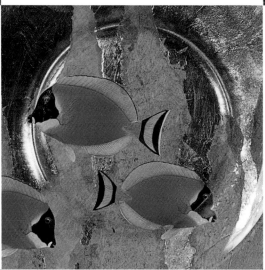
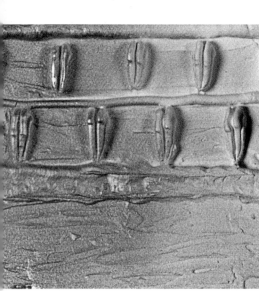

Other Materials

Materials other than paper or fabric, such as glass, metal, or wax, are often viewed as intimidating or too complex to tackle, but common tools and a little bit of guidance can take you down new creative paths. You do not need to be a carpenter, potter, or metalsmith to find success in wood, clay, or wire. Even when working with glass, plaster, or wax, items and tools that you will find no farther away than your backyard or kitchen will set your work apart and assure that it progresses easily. Introduce metal into your work in the form of wire, a material flexible enough to knit or crochet into mesh textures, or strong enough to shape into sculpture. Experiment with new mediums, and combine them with the many techniques you have already mastered to expand the creative possibilities. ✦

Wood presents many options without the use of expensive carpentry tools. The materials needed for a rustic armchair or bench could be just as far away as your backyard.

Thrift shop finds can become "new" antiques with a little patience and elbow grease. Blocks of wood were hammered into the variation to create the impression of years of heavy use. Keep in mind the areas that will be most likely to wear over time.

Photocopying is an easy way to duplicate am image for transferring to wood. Silk-screen copied images of favorite characters or animals to add a touch of whimsy to children's furniture and toys.

turn natural branches into clever insets

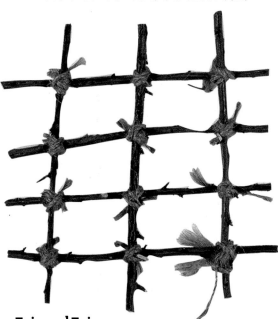

add an aged appearance to new creations

Twigs and Twine

- Sketch out a pattern on paper and carefully select the sticks, twigs, and branches required to complete the design. Make sure that the size and thickness of the branches are suitable for the intended use of the finished piece.

- Lay the sticks out in the pattern, and tie the intersections off with the twine. Make sure the pieces are lashed together very tightly to prevent any movement at their joints.

- Secure the knots in the twine with a dot of glue.

Antiquing Carvings

- Paint the wooden carving with the yellow paint and let it dry overnight before continuing.

- Mix a small amount of burnt umber paint with the yellow, to create a more muted tone. Thin this out with a few drops of water.

- Brush the paint over the surface of the carving and allow it to sit for a few minutes.

- Rub the wet paint off the raised areas of the carving with the rag, leaving the accumulation of burnt umber mixture in the cracks and crevices. This will create the worn appearance. Allow to dry.

materials

- branches
- twine
- saw or garden clippers
- paper
- pencil
- scissors
- PVA glue

- wooden carving
- rag
- yellow acrylic paint
- burnt umber watercolor paint
- paintbrush
- water

branches

The delicate turnings of a branch are highlighted in a design tied off with a very fine wire. Pieces like this are fabulous accents for outdoor furniture, breakfast trays, or window screens.

carving

This sample was slightly banged up before the muted tone of paint was added. It was also sanded with steel wool to wear the paint around its edges.

photocopies become embellishment for wooden projects

Silk Screening

- Make a photocopy of the design, remembering that the finished transfer will be a mirror image of the original.
- Brush a thin coat of screen printing base over the surface of the wood. An application that is too thick will result in the ink being smeared, so test it first.
- Press the image face down into the base on the surface of the wood. Burnish the back of the image thoroughly with your thumb to aid in its transfer. Gently peel back the paper to reveal the picture on the wood. Discard the used photocopy.
- Allow to dry.

image transfer

Color was added after the image was transferred to the wood and it had thoroughly dried. Colored pencils were used in this case, although watercolors work equally well.

- screen printing base
- fresh photocopy of image
- paintbrush
- wooden project

crafter's tip

When using the basic twigs and twine technique, think about where the piece will go. Twine will likely disintegrate if the piece it is used on is left outside year-round. Try using coated wire instead.

Glass seems elegant, yet it is intimidating to think about manipulating it. Personalize your projects with these easy techniques. Etching cream designs embellish glass or mirror surfaces beautifully and add special accents to items such as wedding champagne glasses. Try encasing flowers or invitations in glass for lasting keepsakes.

Shattered glass can seem shocking, but it is a playful twist on the traditional glass used in front doors or room dividers. Substitute an artfully cracked glass in a place where you would normally use glass cubes.

create a simple, elegant etched appearance

display lasting keepsakes

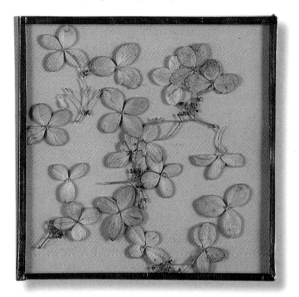

Etching Cream and Glass

○ With the iron set on a medium-low temperature, iron the freezer paper, shiny side down, to the glass. Make sure that the paper has adhered completely to the glass.

○ Sketch the desired pattern in pencil on the freezer paper and cut it out with the craft knife. Peel away portions of the freezer paper to reveal the areas to be treated with the etching cream.

○ Paint a thick coat of etching cream over the entire surface of the glass and let it sit for about ten minutes.

○ Thoroughly rinse off the cream and peel away the remaining freezer paper.

Encasing in Glass

○ Thoroughly clean both sides of each piece of glass. Make sure the glass is dry before continuing.

○ Arrange the flowers on one piece of glass. Carefully place the other glass on top, flattening the encased flowers.

○ While holding the glass firmly in place, run a length of tape along one of the four sides, centering it over the edges of the glass.

○ Fold the tape around and smooth it over the front and back sides of the glass. Trim off any excess tape. Repeat with each of the remaining three sides.

materials

■ freezer paper
■ iron
■ glass
■ etching cream
■ paintbrush
■ water
■ craft knife
■ pencil

■ two identical pieces of glass
■ metal foil tape
■ dried flowers
■ scissors
■ glass cleaner
■ rag

etch

Simple striping creates a more structured design than the swirls of the project. Try a monogram pattern for a personalized accent.

brute force generates graceful lines

encase

To encase three-dimensional objects, create a box from glass by cutting sides to the required height and assembling them as described in the project. This is a perfect way to display awards or a child's first pair of shoes.

Shattered Glass

- Clean the glass before beginning.

- On a sturdy work surface, place the laminated glass between the two felts to prevent glass shards from spraying about. Whenever you work with glass, take appropriate measures to protect your hands and eyes.

- Firmly smack the glass through the top felt with the hammer. The more it is hammered, the finer and denser the crack lines in the glass will be.

- Carefully remove the glass from the felts; the glass will be cracked, but it will still be intact. Sweep off any remaining glass shards. Wash the felts and vacuum your work area to ensure that there are no glass pieces.

shatter

Instead of multiple hits to the glass, the spider web design of this piece was created by one sharp smack of the hammer. Try using tile-sized pieces of glass for an unusual table top.

- laminated glass
- two felts or towels
- hammer
- small broom
- dustpan
- rag
- glass cleaner
- sturdy work surface
- washing machine
- dryer
- vacuum cleaner

crafter's tip

▲ When working with etching cream, protect the back side of the glass by applying a sheet of freezer paper to it as described in the project.

Metal is generally assumed to be a difficult material, which is all the more reason to bring it into your work in the form of wire. There are a wide variety of thicknesses and types that can be combined, used alone, or even coated with spray paint.

Wire can add a bold statement or a delicate overtone to your work. Fine wires crocheted into overlays or twisted into jewelry leave a very elegant impression. Heavy-gauge wires can be manipulated into baskets or faux wrought-iron candleholders.

making decorative fabric with metal

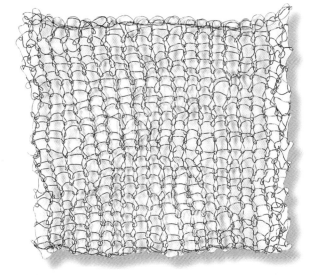

fashion a kind of decorative armor

Knitting Wire

- Choose a lightweight copper wire, such as twenty-six gauge, and a pair of knitting needles in an appropriate size. The ones used here are a size nine. For larger or smaller stitches, adjust the needle size accordingly.

- Be aware that wires that are too thin may break, and wires that are too heavy will be difficult to bend.

- Cast on the stitches as in regular knitting.

- To form this stockinet stitch, knit a row of stitches followed by a row of purled stitches, just as you would if you were working with yarn. Continue in this manner until the swatch is finished.

Chain Mail

- Using the pliers, create two chains of rings in an alternating pattern of a single ring linked through two rings, linked through one ring.

- Lay the two chains side by side on the foam core and pin them down. Make sure that the double rings from each chain line up with one another, as do the single rings.

- Use two jump rings to connect two corresponding single jump rings. Continue until the chains are connected.

- Repeat the entire process until the piece is the required size.

- Be sure the rings are fully closed to prevent any of them from slipping apart.

materials

- lightweight copper wire
- knitting needles
- wire cutters

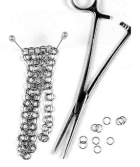

- 7mm jump rings
- surgical pliers or needle-nosed pliers
- pins
- foam core
- 7mm jump rings

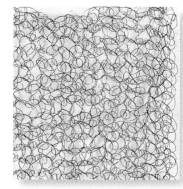

crochet

A thread-like steel wire was crocheted into a fine mesh that would be wonderful as an addition to evening bags or lantern shades. Try incorporating beads or sequins for added dazzle.

artistic shapes from metal

chains

There are numerous traditional chain mail designs to try out; this one demonstrates a European four-in-one pattern. Try using chain mail to create gothic home accessories such as sconces and room dividers.

Sculpting with Wire

○ Determine the shape and form of the finished piece by sketching it on paper. Keep in mind what the use of the project will be so you have a practical design to apply to it.

○ With the sketch as a guide, use the pliers to hold and bend the wire into shape.

○ You may find that it is easier to measure off and mark the wire with tiny dots to note the exact location of bends, turns, or twists. Use a sharp pencil or an erasable pen so the markings can be easily removed upon completion of the piece.

sculpt

Combine different gauge wires in one project, such as this twisted crosspiece figure. Wire sculptures can be sharp and angular or incorporate soft, playful curves and swirls.

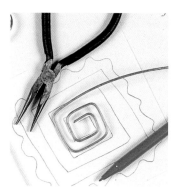

- ■ 12-gauge wire
- ■ pliers
- ■ white paper
- ■ pencil
- ■ wire cutters
- ■ pen

crafter's tip

▲ To create a traditional chain mail piece, form coils resembling springs from heavy-gauge wire by wrapping it around a steel dowel. Cut the coils of the spring apart so that you have what will look like open jump rings.

R arely is decoupage considered a medium for precious metals. Combining gold leaf with organic papers, however, produces breathtaking results. Manipulate the gold leaf further by scratching or shattering the leaf. Experiment with both artificial and real gold leaf to explore their differences, or introduce silver leaf instead.

Metalsmithing is one of the most ancient art forms, its appeal being rooted in its long history. The tools for both of these simple metalwork procedures are available at metal shops and hardware stores. With a little practice, you will be forming your own jewelry, screens, and sculptures.

easily apply a rich finish

cutouts create distinctive silhouettes

Gold Leaf Decoupage

- Apply the glue over the front sides of the images and rice paper strips. Arrange them face down, one layer at a time, on the back side of the piece and burnish thoroughly. Let each layer dry.
- For other projects, the decoupage may need to be adhered to the front of the piece.
- Apply the gold size to the back of the plate with a clean brush. Refer to manufacturer's specifications for drying times.
- Lay gold leaf sheets over the areas to be covered. Brush off any that do not adhere.
- Trim off the overhang from the images and gold leaf. Lightly sand the edge of plate until it is smooth to the touch.

Piercing Metal

- If desired, texture the surface of the copper with 36-grain sandpaper.
- Sketch a design on paper and adhere it to the metal with the rubber cement.
- Drill holes in the areas that will be removed from the pattern.
- Thread the blade of the saw through a hole, making sure that the blade's teeth point down. Clamp the pin to the work surface, and rest the copper on top of it. Carefully saw along pattern lines.
- Peel off the pattern and rub off the cement. File cut edges with needle files, and then sand with the emery paper until smooth.

materials

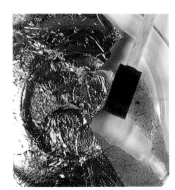

- artificial gold leaf
- quick-drying size
- decoupage glue
- images
- Japanese rice papers torn into strips
- sponge brushes
- craft knife
- sandpaper
- glass plate or project to be treated

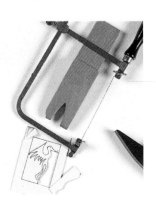

- copper sheet metal
- jeweler's saw and saw blades
- notched wooden pin
- clamp
- paper
- pen
- rubber cement
- needle files
- emery paper
- hand drill
- sandpaper

gold leaf
Displays, such as these on this beautiful charger, prove that gold leaf applications do not need to be limited to picture frames and furniture. Try this technique on unusual objects such as buttons, windows, and planters.

add form and texture to metal rods

pierce
A sample makes use of the negative instead of the positive space. To create the surface finish, use a torch to slowly heat the copper, allowing the colorful oxides to form.

Cold Metal Forging

○ Holding the rod steady with the vice, cut the rod and heat until it is red hot. Let cool.

○ Place it in the pickle until the oxides, discoloration caused by the annealing process (heating and cooling), are gone. Remove from the pickle and clean with brush and soap.

○ Lay the rod on the anvil and shape with the hammer. Both ends of a riveting hammer achieved these different textures.

○ To continue shaping the rod after it becomes hard, repeat the above processes.

○ If forming a bracelet, hammer the rod around a stake with the mallet.

○ File and sand until smooth, progressing from rough to fine grits.

forge
A brass rod gracefully loops into a simple and elegant formation. Try designing your own handles, finials, and coat hooks.

- 1/4" (.5 cm) round copper rod
- jeweler's or coping saw
- anvil
- forging or riveting hammer
- plastic mallet
- vice
- torch
- emery paper
- file
- pickle (sulfuric acid and water)
- bucket
- wire brush
- dish soap
- stake

crafter's tip

▲ When checking the tackiness of the gold size, use a knuckle instead of fingertips to avoid leaving oil imprints from the skin.

Ceramics, although beautiful, just beg for embellishment. Materials are readily available through craft and tile stores or by mail order; the electric kiln required will be easy to find and is but a modest purchase. Alternately, professional and educational studios will frequently rent out space in their kilns for firings.

Mosaics are a lovely way to recycle leftover tiles or broken china, and the basic supplies needed are available at hardware stores. Experiment with the range of colored grouts to best complement your project.

make custom tiles with ease

recycle pieces of tile to form a masterpiece

Hand-painting Tiles

○ Sketch the design on the tile in pencil.

○ Fill in the design, applying the glazes with a paintbrush.

○ After the colored glazes have dried, brush a coat of clear glaze over the surface of the tile. It is important to wipe the back side of the tile with a damp sponge to remove any drips.

○ Gradually fire the tile and cone in the kiln: one hour set at low, one hour at medium, and then on high until the cone 05 melts enough to bend in half.

○ Remove the tile from the kiln when it is cool to the touch.

Mosaics

○ Sketch the design on paper, and copy it directly onto the wood's surface.

○ Cut the tile into small pieces. Arrange these within the paper design.

○ Apply a coat of mastic with the putty knife, as directed, over a small portion of the wood blank. Press the corresponding tile pieces into place. Continue until the design is completed. Set aside for twenty-four to forty-eight hours to dry.

○ Protect necessary areas from the grout with masking tape. Prepare the grout as directed and pour it over the tiles. Squeegee off the excess.

○ With a damp sponge, wipe off the tiles. Let dry for at least a day.

materials

■ biscuit commercial tile or hand-crafted tile

■ paintbrushes

■ pencil

■ colored and clear glazes

■ electric kiln

■ cone 05

■ sponge

■ water

■ wood blank

■ tile mastic (adhesive)

■ tile

■ tile nippers

■ tile cutter (optional)

■ squeegee

■ sponge

■ water

■ wall grout

■ tracing paper

■ masking tape

■ permanent marker

■ pencil

■ plastic putty knife

This hand-painted tile is also handmade. The clay was rolled to a thickness of 1/4" (.5 cm) and then carved with ceramic tools. After the tile was biscuit-fired and dry, it was painted and fired again.

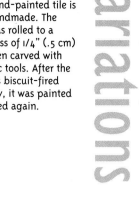

shells create a more delicate tile

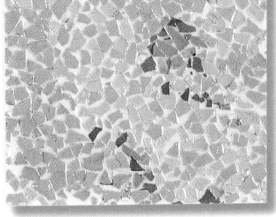

 mosaics

Do not let store selections of tile limit your design possibilities. This mosaic features tiles that were hand-painted before being nipped into shape.

Eggshell Mosaics

- Remove their linings and let the eggshells soak for several minutes in the dye until they have become an appealing color.
- Sketch out the design on the surface of the project. Brush a thin coat of glue over a small area, and press small pieces of eggshell into place. Tweezers will make handling the pieces easier. Continue in this manner until the design has been filled in.
- After several hours, when the glue has dried, brush a thick coat of acrylic medium over the piece with a foam brush. After each coat dries, apply another until the surface is level.

eggshells

Large patches of cracked shell with wide gaps in-between create a reptilian feel in a surprising medium. Experiment with color values and backgrounds to test design options.

- pale eggshells
- fabric dyes
- small container
- PVA glue
- acrylic medium
- glue brush
- tweezers
- foam brush
- pencil
- fabric or paper

crafter's tip

▲ If any portion of a finished painted tile is unsatisfactory, touch it up with additional glaze and refire.

Icing with drywall plaster gives a craftsperson with no carpentry skills the ability to create finely detailed cornice work or delicate reliefs on almost any surface. Bring elegance to thrift store finds such as furniture, frames, and boxes.

More home and garden items than you would expect can be treated with the yogurt aging technique. Planters, birdbaths, and even walkways and paths can look as though they have been part of the landscape for years. Try this on terra cotta, brick, concrete, slate, or stone.

cake-decorating tools easily form plaster designs

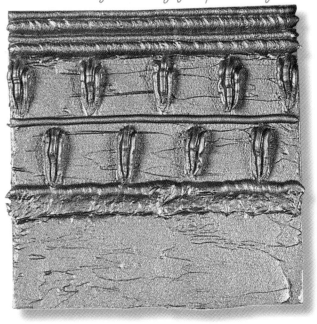

Icing with Plaster

- Spread a generous layer of plaster over the surface with the butter knife as if you are icing a cake. Let this base application dry overnight before adding the next stage of plaster.
- Choose an appropriate tip for the icing bag to create the pattern you wish to achieve.
- With the spoon, fill the icing bag with drywall plaster that is free of lumps. Work the plaster down toward the bottom of the bag to eliminate any pockets of air.

- Try a test swatch to make sure the pattern is clear. If you find that the plaster "melts" into an indistinct bead, allow it to sit out for about an hour with the icing bag open so it may dry slightly. Try a test swatch again before continuing.
- Form the desired pattern on the piece just as you would if you were icing a cake. Avoid very thick applications of plaster so it will not crack as it dries. Allow the plaster to dry thoroughly before treating with a surface finish such as paint.

materials

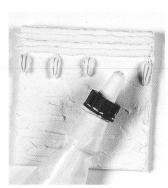

- drywall plaster
- icing bag and an assortment of tips
- surface to decorate
- paint
- spoon or spatula
- butter knife
- test swatches

organic substances add to nature's bounty

plaster

A basket weave effect created by a flat, ridged icing tip adds a wonderful texture to this picture frame.

aged terra cotta

A terra-cotta plant pot was treated with the yogurt to bring out mossy tones of green and gray. The contrast with the burnt umber of the terra cotta is especially appealing.

Aging Stone

- Select a plain yogurt with active cultures such as bifidus and/or acidophilus. You can also try working with whole milk or cream.
- Brush a generous layer of the yogurt over the surface of the stone, allowing it to accumulate in the cracks and crevices.
- Set the stone outside in a moist, partially shaded location. High humidity will speed up the process. It will take several weeks, but various lichens and mosses will start to grow over the surface of the stone, giving it an aged and mottled tone.

- plain yogurt
- stone
- foam brush

crafter's tip

▲ To color the drywall plaster before you decorate with it, make a very strong solution of liquid dye and mix it into the plaster. You will probably have to allow the mixture to dry out back to its original consistency before using it.

Wax is an ancient substance that may seem to offer little that is exciting and original, yet these two techniques present new options. Treasured keepsakes can be beautifully preserved and displayed in wax, or a wax tile can become the playful centerpiece of a table or book cover when protected by glass.

Elegant wax leaves are so simple to make, yet their outcome is striking. Use them to decorate boxes and cakes, or create a larger arrangement to become a framed piece.

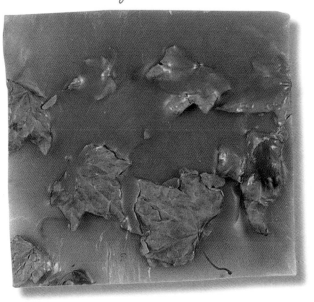

embedding items in hot wax

Objects in Wax

- Fill the pot halfway with water, and place a sheet of tin foil over the top of the pot. Push the center of the tin foil down until it just touches the surface of the water. This will act as a hammock to suspend the tin can. Place the pot on the stove and bring the water to a boil.

- Break the wax into small pieces and put them in the tin can. Place this over the heat. Stirring the wax will help it to melt more quickly.

- While the wax is melting, spray the shallow pan with cooking spray so the cool wax will be able to be removed easily. Randomly scatter the leaves over the tray.

- When the wax is thoroughly melted, use the tongs to lift the can off the tin foil and pour the wax over the leaves in the pan. Be sure that the pan is on a level surface.

- When the wax achieves a butter-like consistency, cut it into the desired shape. Gently remove it from the pan when it is thoroughly cool.

materials

- beeswax
- tin can
- tin foil
- cooking pot
- water
- stove
- dried ivy leaves
- shallow pan

- cooking spray
- stirring stick
- tongs
- knife

elegant structures made of brushed wax

wax display

Stamps and coins are artfully displayed in a sample featuring various travel memorabilia. Be sure that any objects used for this technique can withstand the temperature of hot wax.

leaf colors

By using several different colors of wax on one leaf, a New England autumn has been preserved, in part. The actual leaf itself served as the color guide.

Wax Leaves

- Melt the wax as described in Objects in Wax. To color the beeswax, add small pieces of crayon.
- Select fresh, thick leaves with strong vein patterns. Thoroughly wash and dry them.
- When the wax is melted, brush an even coat over one side of a leaf. Make sure the wax is thick enough to keep it from breaking easily.
- Place the leaf in the refrigerator for several minutes to cool the wax.
- Starting at the stem, gently peel back and remove the leaf from the wax. You may be able to use the same leaf at least once more.

- beeswax
- crayons
- assortment of leaves
- small paintbrush
- tin can
- tin foil
- cooking pot
- water
- stove
- towel
- refrigerator

crafter's safety tip

▲ If you should overheat the wax to the point that a fire ignites, never use water to put it out. That will cause the fire to spread. Instead, smother the flames or pour baking soda over them.

Experiments in Wood

 The grain in wood can capture inks strongly, adding to the cloudy quality of shadowed or silhouetted figures. Protect the images with several coats of varnish or polyurethane.

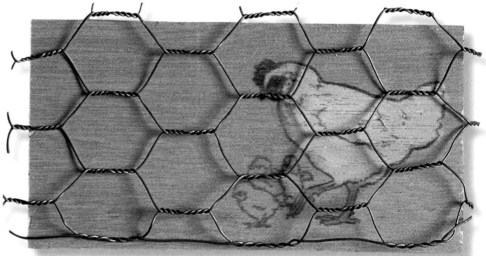 Try combining and layering different types of materials and images to create the overall design. Pieces such as this are great for cabinet doors and trunk lids.

 Grapes and vine tendrils are washed with watercolors for a soft effect. As long as the surface of the wood does not have a gloss finish, any liquid coloring may be used.

Experiments in Glass

Glass panels, etched with fruits or vegetables, make wonderful insets for kitchen cabinets. Design a set of glass plates, bowls, and glasses to match the theme.

Etched patterns work well as a background or as the subject itself. Create a beautiful visual protector with allover designs for glass in front doors and side lights.

Playful figures are the perfect accent to have tiptoeing across the borders of a child's mirror or bath. Try etched designs on colored glass as well.

Experiments in Sculpted Wire

 Rolling waves formed by twisted copper and nickel wire provide a playground for swimming friends. Any number of other items could be incorporated into wire creations. Experiment with fresh or dried flowers, lentils, or buttons.

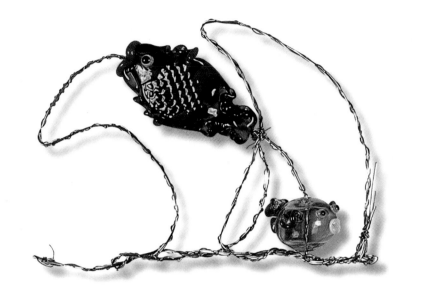

 A swirled design incorporates small pieces of amethyst that were threaded onto and braided with the wire. Test your design skills with delicate jewelry and hair decoration projects.

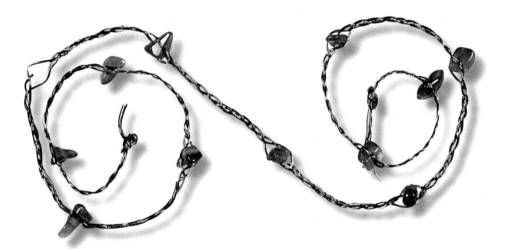

 These beads give this sample the look of a very elegant abacus. Expanding on this idea, beautiful baskets, serving trays, and room dividers may also be fashioned.

Experiments in Metal

To quickly age and add character to metal projects, soak them with household liquids, such as water or vinegar. Here, brass, copper, tin, glavanized steel, and cold-rolled steel samples were soaked in bleach.

Bleach

Combine ammonia with the same metals to produce a verdigis effect, perfect for finishing metal flower pots, chimes, or garden sculptures.

Ammonia

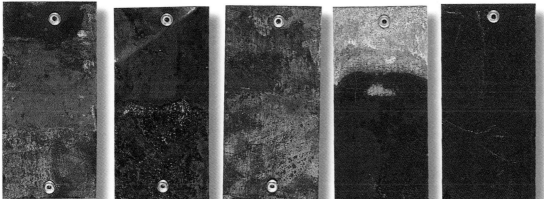

A household cleaner, applied to brass or copper, creates a colorful patina of age and texture.

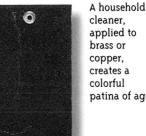

safety tip

▲ When working with chemicals, make sure your work area is well-ventilated and prohibit smoking. Wear gloves and goggles, and protect all work surfaces.

Toilet Bowl Cleaner

Experiments in Mosaics

 Broken pottery recycles into a beautiful tile piece. Sand was rubbed into the wet plaster to create a beach-like feel against the seashell tones of the pottery.

 Mosaics of mixed beans make unusual tiles for kitchen walls, coasters, and trays. Varnishes and liquid plastics are perfect for finishing and protecting the pieces.

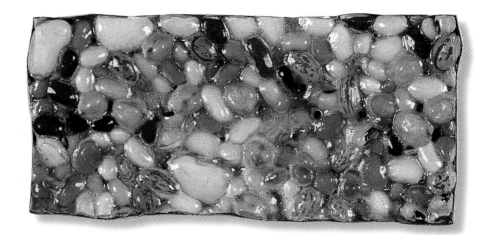

 Do not be limited to tiles in fashioning mosaics. Just about anything can be incorporated into the designs. Here, stray puzzle pieces find a new life.

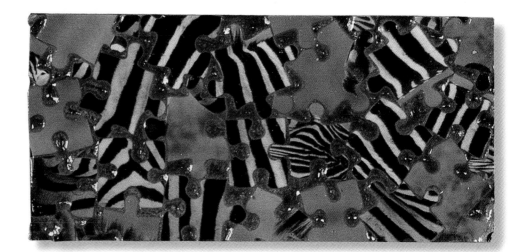

Experiments in Plaster

Any number of tools can be used to texture a plaster finish. This sample was formed with an adhesive spreader, then colored with four different tones of purple.

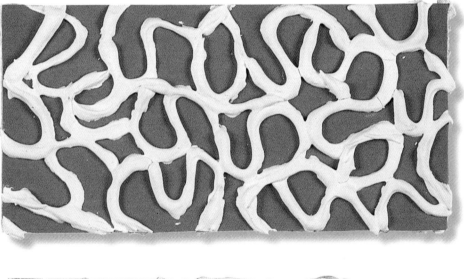

A funky lacework pattern makes a fun accent for chair backs and baskets.  Try forming the beads of plaster with different tips to incorporate a variety of textures.

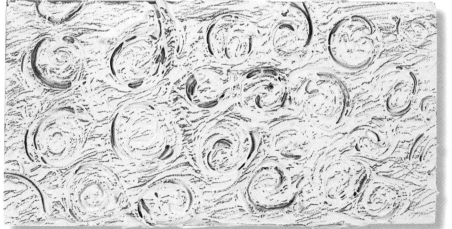

Swirls were made in the wet plaster with a stylus, and it was then allowed to dry. Purple pencil was gently rubbed over the surface to accentuate the texture.

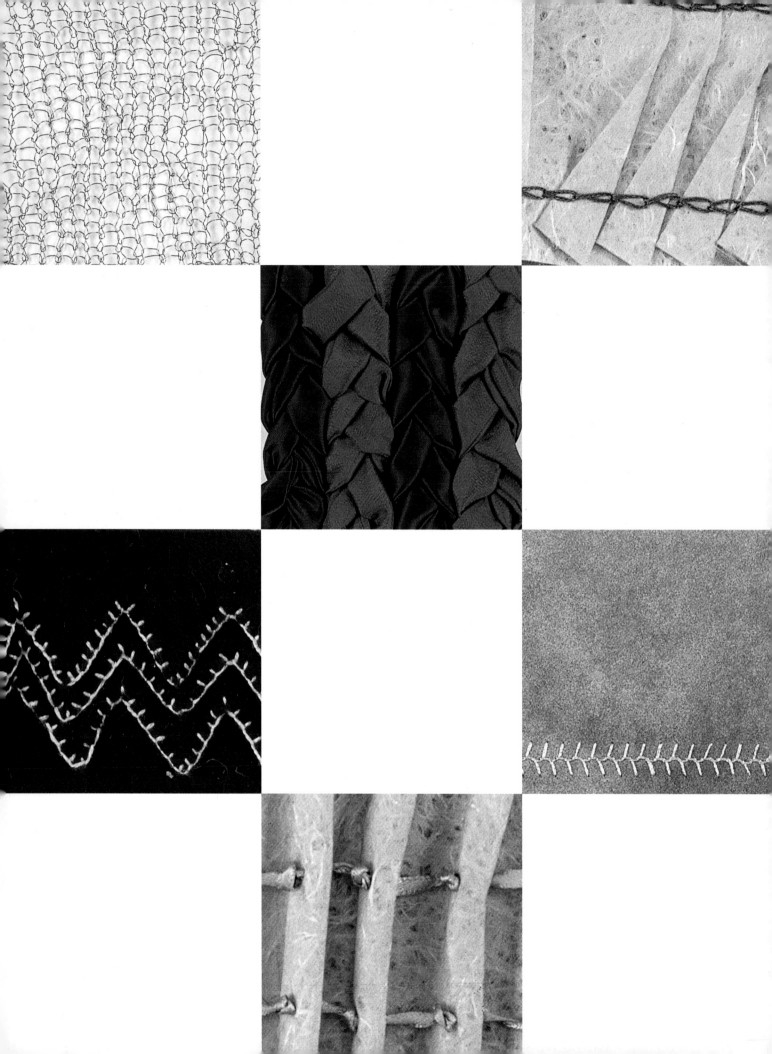

Recipe Resources

Creating beautiful craft projects requires only the right tools, inspiring materials, and a knowledge of a few, versatile skills. This resource section supplies most of the basic instruction for stitching, knitting, and braiding that you will need to complete the various recipes in *The Crafter's Recipe Book*. Look to these, and to the patterns and stencils that follow, when first getting acquainted with the crafting process, or when designing your own projects.

Remember to take your time and experiment. A simple change of material, scale, or color can lead to unexpected motifs, textures, and perceived depths. Start with the basics, and soon your work room will become a gallery of inspirations. ✦

Sewing Stitches

 The running stitch is a very basic stitch and involves no more than moving the needle in and out of the fabric at even intervals.

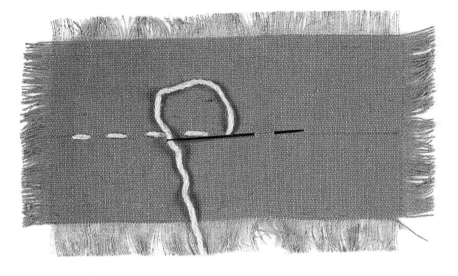

There are dozens of decorative stitches, one of the easiest being the chain stitch. Experiment with different weights and types of thread, yarn, and floss for a variety of results.

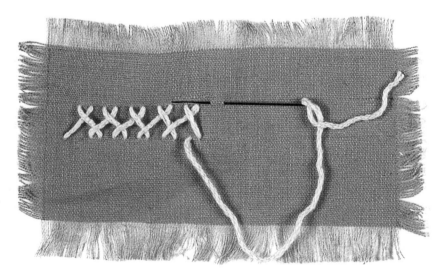

 A series of *X* s line up next to and overlap one another in a regular herringbone pattern. Try capturing lines of text beneath the stitches.

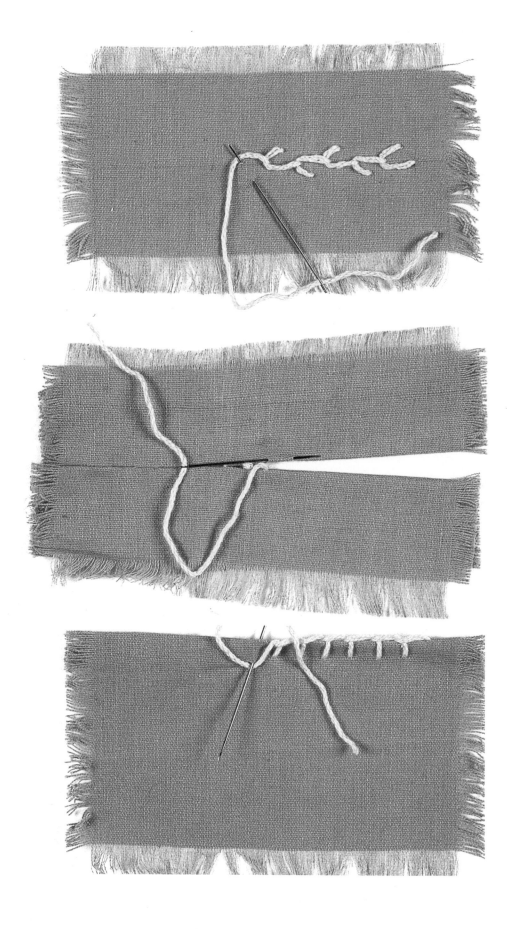

The feather stitch is based on the same premise as the chain stitch; the thread is caught and formed into shape with the needle.

Fold under the edges of the two pieces of fabric that will be joined. Take a stitch along the fold line of one piece of fabric. Start the next stitch by inserting the needle in the other fold, directly opposite the exit point of the first stitch. Keep the needle traveling along the two fold lines, without catching any other part of the fabric. With each stitch, the thread is caught beneath the fabric, hidden from view.

Used as decorative edging on items such as blankets, cuffs, and mufflers, the buttonhole or blanket stitch handsomely accents the work while also providing a finished edge.

Knitting

- Make a noose by curving the end of the yarn back over itself. Pull the yarn through the resulting loop and tighten.

- Slide the noose over the left knitting needle. Slip the right needle through it, from the bottom and behind the left needle. From the back side of the work, wrap the loose end of the yarn around the right needle, and pull it in-between the two tools.

- Pull the yarn through the noose loop with the right needle. Transfer the stitch back to the left needle. Continue casting on until enough stitches have been formed for your project.

- Begin a knitting row by forming a stitch in the same manner as when casting on. This time, the new stitch will remain on the right needle, and the stitch from the previous row is dropped from the left needle.

- The stockinet stitch in these samples is created with alternating rows of knit and purl stitches. To purl, insert the right needle through a stitch on the left needle, from top to bottom on the left needle's front side.

- From the front side of the work, bring the yarn over and around the right needle. Pull the yarn through the stitch on the left needle, forming a new one on the right. Release the stitch from the left tool.

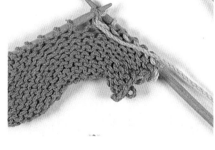

- Casting off can be done on either a knit or purl row. Begin by forming two stitches as usual. With the left needle, pull the first stitch formed over the second, off the point of the right needle. Continue until all stitches have been cast off.

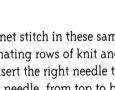

Align two ribbons side by side. Weave the third under and over the first two, forming a right angle.

Fold the yellow ribbon over to the right to run parallel to the purple ribbon.

Fold the purple ribbon to the left so it is parallel to the pink ribbon.

Repeat the process of folding each ribbon into place, proceeding next to the pink ribbon, then back to the yellow and purple ribbons until you reach the end.

Stencils

Use these stencils to make your own recipe designs. Make sure you cut inside the solid lines to create the stencil shape. To make a sturdier, long-lasting stencil, photocopy these designs onto cardstock, or glue the copied stencils to cardboard and cut out.

Stencils

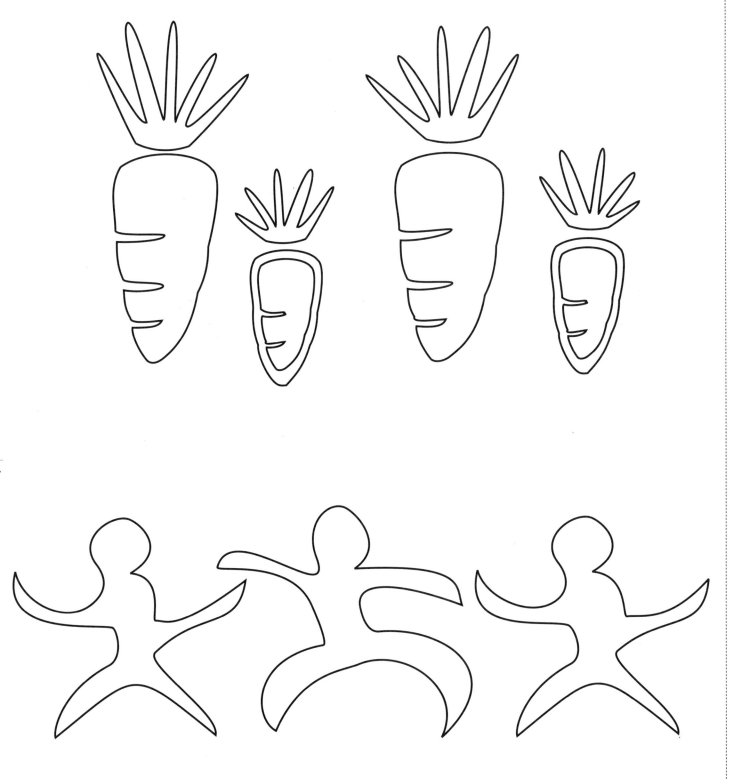

Patterns

Scale pattern: ——— Cut   ------- Fold

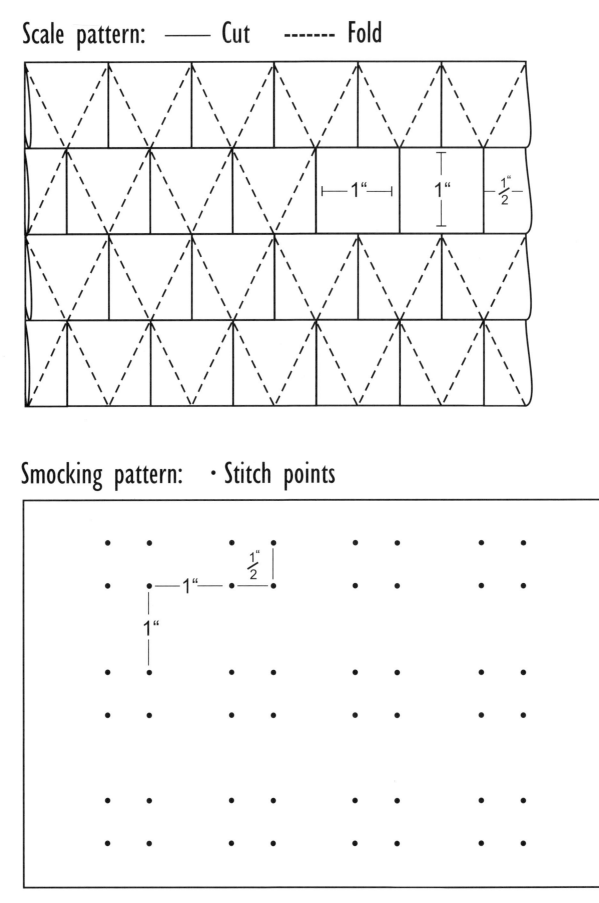

Smocking pattern: · Stitch points

Cutwork Pattern (Cut away white section)

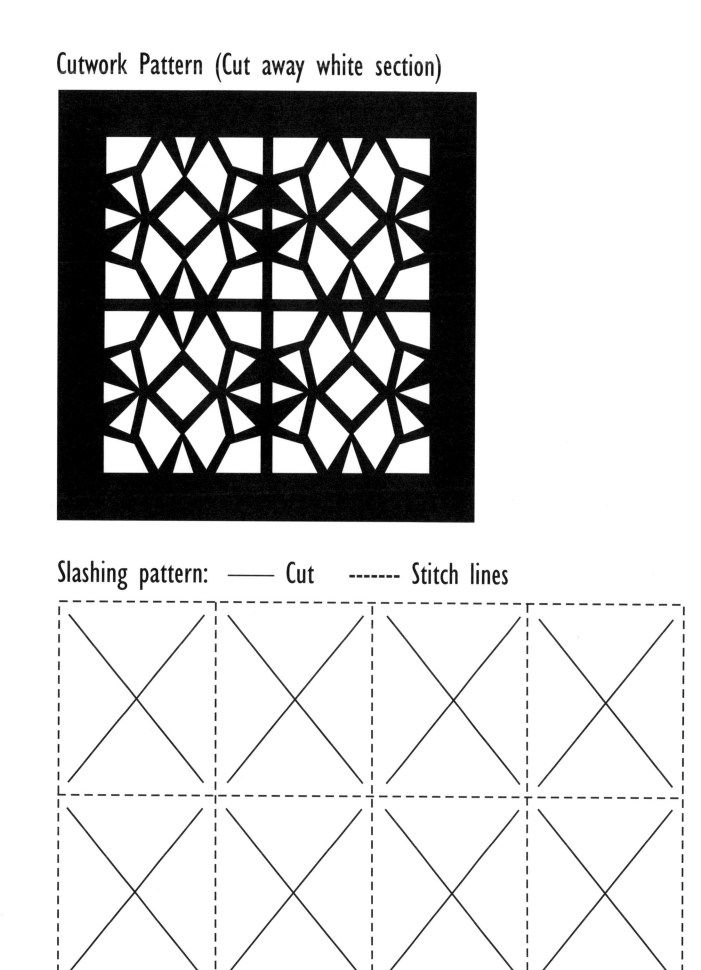

Slashing pattern: ——— Cut ------- Stitch lines

Patterns

Paper folding pattern

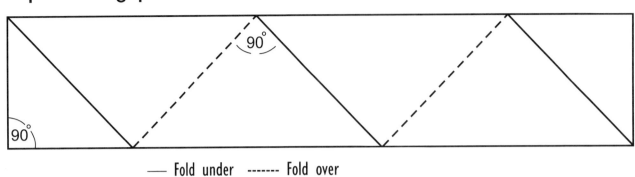

—— Fold under   ------- Fold over

Paper folding variation pattern

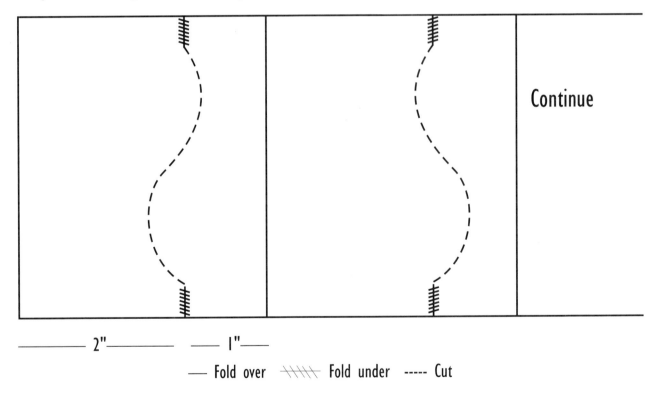

Continue

—— 2"——   —— 1"——

—— Fold over   //////// Fold under   ----- Cut

Stippling pattern (In-step stitches)

Stippling pattern (Out-of-step stitches)

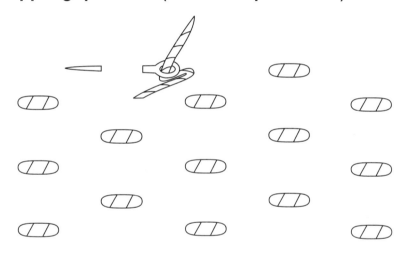

Stippling pattern (arched stitches)

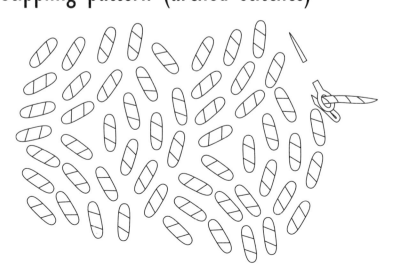

Contributors

Clipping Nap Fabrics (page 80)

Thomas Soderberg
14 Carpenter Street
Salem, MA 01970

Freelance illustration and costume design.

Crayon Batik (page 40),
Bubble Marbling (page 41)

Paula Beardell Krieg
6087 State Route 22
Salem, NY 12865

An accomplished artist, Paula teaches book arts extensively in the New York area.

Decoupage Designs (page 14)

Cathy McLaurin
Chest
c/o Amesbury Artworks
10 R Street
Amesbury, MA 01913
978-388-5954
cathyr@greennet.com

Cathy is the owner/artist behind Chest, a business that designs and decoupages one-of-a-kind boxes out of her studio in Amesbury, Massachusetts.

Experiments in Metal (page 123)

Jarred Sadowski
Port Sheet Metal
154 State Street
Newburyport, MA 01950
978-462-6132

Port Sheet Metal carries sheet metal and other supplies.

Experiments in Sculpted Wire (page 122)

Charlotte Sorsen
10 R Street
Amesbury, MA 01913
978-388-5954

A glass bead artist, Charlotte handmakes and custom designs glass beads, jewelry, and accessories.

Fabric Constructions (page 101)

Sam Kimball
65 Highland Street
Amesbury, MA 01913
978-388-8758

Figurative and abstract oil painting.

Gocco Printing (page 93)

Mary McCarthy
249 A Street #25
Boston, MA 02210
617-695-0688

Author of Making Books by Hand, *Mary creates one-of-a-kind artist books and accepts numerous commissions.*

For more information on Gocco printing or to order a Print Gocco Kit, call 978-739-3523, e-mail to azuppa@riso.com, or visit the Gocco website at http://www.gocco.com.

Gold Leaf Decoupage (page 112)

Edith Heyck
Newburyport, MA
978-462-9027

Edith combines her knowledge of gold leaf gilding with exotic Japanese rice papers and natural images to create alluring heirloom plates. She is currently teaching "The Joy of Creativity" at her studio.

Hand-painting Tiles (page 114)

Bay James
51 Plum Island Turnpike
Newbury, MA 01951
phone 978-465-1921
fax 978-463-0554
saltydog@seacoast.com

Bay James specializes in unique tile murals for home or industry. She also customizes premanufactured vanity sets to coordinate with original or existing settings.

Mosaics *(page 114)*

Bridgette Heidi Newfell
10 Orange Street
Newburyport, MA 01950
978-465-5969

Bridgette designs and creates unique textile and mosaic art.

Rugg Road Paper Company
105 Charles Street
Boston, MA 02114
617-742-0002

Photo Emulsions *(page 90)*

Tara Wrobel
P.O. Box 732
West Newbury, MA 01985

Tara is an accomplished fine arts photographer. Inquiries about her work are welcome.

Piercing Metal *(page 112),*
Cold Metal Forging *(page 113)*

Kathleen Batcheller
Millie's Mighty Metal Shop
10 R Street
Amesbury, MA 01913
978-463-7767

Kathleen's metalwork explores the influences of Mother Nature and human nature in movement, symbols, and emotion.

Recipe Resources: Knitting *(page 130)*

Charlotte's Web
Exeter Village Shops
137 Epping Road
Exeter, NH 03833
888-244-6460 (toll free)

Exeter Village Shops specializes in fine yarns.

Rubber Stamping *(page 95)*

Ferther and Moore Rubber Stamps
P. O. Box 732
West Newbury, MA 01985

A catalog of original art rubber stamps is available upon request.

Rug Hooking *(page 82)*

Annie A. Spring
22 Clark's Road
Amesbury, MA 01913
978-388-0209

Annie is an instructor of traditional rug hooking.

Silk Painting *(page 87)*

Lucinda Cathcart
Chameleon: An Ever-changing Collection
   of Fine Art and Objects
22 Liberty Street
Newburyport, MA 01950
978-463-7623

Lucinda hand-paints all her silks, combining her strong graphic design training with a passion for color and form that is inspired by the beauty of things in everyday life.

Index

About the Author

Jessica Wrobel's studio work encompasses a range of paper,
fiber, floral, and creative package design along with specialties
such as handcrafted books, boxes, albums, and fine art papers.
Jessica and her husband Tom Eaton are also involved in
numerous projects that further the arts in their community.

Jessica Wrobel
West Newbury, MA
978-363-2106
jwrobel@seacoast.com